Managing Your Time

Managing
Your Time

*What to do and how to do it
in order to do more*

JULIE-ANN AMOS

How To Books

By the same author in this series

Managing Yourself
Starting to Manage

Published by How To Books Ltd, 3 Newtec Place,
Magdalen Road, Oxford OX4 1RE. United Kingdom.
Tel: (01865) 793806. Fax: (01865) 248780.
email: info@howtobooks.co.uk
www.howtobooks.co.uk

British Library Cataloguing in Publication Data
A catalogue record for this book is available from
the British Library

Cover design by Shireen Nathoo Design
Cover image PhotoDisc
Cartoons by Mike Flanagan

Produced for How To Books by Deer Park Productions
Typeset by PDQ Typesetting, Stoke-on-Trent, Staffs.
Printed and bound by Cromwell Press, Trowbridge, Wiltshire

NOTE: The material contained in this book is set out in good faith for
general guidance and no liability can be accepted for loss or expense incurred
as a result of relying in particular circumstances on statements made in the
book. Laws and regulations are complex and liable to change, and readers
should check the current position with the relevant authorities before making
personal arrangements.

Contents

List of Illustrations

Preface

Ask any retired person what they would do differently if they had their life to live again. Not many of them would say 'spend more time at the office'.

We are all busy people. Regardless of the type of work we do, more and more of the time, people are feeling crowded in by events. Making busy and/or hectic lives manageable is therefore a skill which almost everyone can benefit from.

This book aims to give you sound advice, hints and tips for managing what you do with your time. The majority of suggestions given here aren't major. No one is talking about making huge changes to the way you work. If you just changed a dozen small things, you would end up with quite a substantial change overall, as the cumulative effect of the changes adds up.

Each chapter concentrates on a different area associated with time management, and there are questions and answers to help you understand the points covered. At the end of each chapter is a checklist, and discussion points to help you relate what you have read to your unique circumstances. Finally, I have included case studies in each chapter, showing three very different, interrelated people, and how they manage their time (or mismanage it!).

I hope from this that you will find it easier to control events and workloads, and start to feel more in control of your time.

Julie-Ann Amos

1
Understanding Time

UNDERSTANDING TIME'S IMPORTANCE

Time may be infinite, but each one of us only has a finite allocation: time is something you can't increase or decrease. No matter how clever you are, how wealthy, how industrious, you still get 24 hours, 1,440 minutes, 86,400 seconds in each and every day, no more, no less. So 'time management' is a misnomer; a fallacy; a **lie**. Time simply can't be managed! You can't:

- control it
- increase it
- decrease it
- speed it up
- slow it down
- extend it.

So why do so many books, training programmes, etc. talk about time management? Well, what they are really talking about is time **usage** – managing the **use** to which you put your time.

Time is like a box, with 24 hours of space in it. Every day when you open it up, it has 24 hours of space in it again, regardless of what space you left empty in it yesterday: whether or not you used it all. You can't swop the box for one bigger or smaller, because everybody's box is exactly the same size! And you can't use anyone's box but your own.

Now do you get the idea? You may even have begun to see the biggest time management problem for most people – **you don't always start with an empty box**.

What you have is a conveyor belt of boxes, one for each day. Every day, some of the contents (the things you scheduled to do) left over in the box get piled up in tomorrow's box, along with all the things you chose to put in there for tomorrow. Every activity you commit to is eating into the space, lurking to surprise you when you open the box up. No wonder we get so crowded in by events, and wish for a bigger box!

But even if someone could wave a magic wand, and give you an extra couple of hours in each day, you'd soon fill them! Before long, we would all be back to square one. What you need to do is to carefully manage the time you've got, putting it to the best use possible.

UNDERSTANDING TIME MANAGEMENT'S IMPORTANCE

Before you can save time, you have to spend some. You have to understand time management and make a little effort to do things like:

- plan
- organise
- review
- rearrange
- sort
- think
- even read this book.

Investing time in time management is one of the best investments you can make. The word 'invest' means to give something, in the expectation of getting more back in return. We all know what investing money means, but do we ever talk about investing time? No – the phrase we usually use is **spending** time, rather than talking about investing it. In a nutshell, time management is a lot about investing more time, and spending less.

In fact, notice how most of the words commonly used about time are money-orientated:

- buying time
- losing time
- making time

- saving time

- spending time

- wasting time.

But time *isn't* money – you *can't* make it, or save it. Time is even more important: because you can use time to make money, but no amount of money can buy you one extra second of time. In fact, time becomes more valuable the less of it we have: it's like most commodities.

So managing your time (or more accurately, managing how you use your time) is one of the most important things you can do.

Good time management
Good time management can:

- give you more time to do what you want

- improve your availability

- improve your decision-making

- improve your health

- improve your productivity, efficiency, effectiveness

- make you easier to live with

- make you easier to work with

- make you feel more relaxed

- minimise the risks you take

- reduce stress

and a lot more besides!

SETTING LIMITS

Good time management is all about setting limits. You need to set all sorts of limits to manage your time well. Set limits for:

- availability (how willing you are to be disturbed, to make yourself **available** for others, etc.)

- duration (how **long** you spend doing things)

- importance (how you **prioritise** things)
- involvement (how much you do **yourself** as opposed to delegate to others)
- standards (how **well** you do things)
- urgency (how **quickly** you do things).

Let's take each of these in turn and see how your time management can be improved by setting limits.

Limiting availability
When the phone rings and someone asks us something, or when someone walks in the door, we very often stop what we're doing and deal with it. What makes these interruptions so urgent? Just because someone asks us something, it doesn't make giving a reply more important or urgent than what we were in the middle of doing. We're conditioned to *react*, and often this means dealing with things as if they were more necessary than they really are. You don't have to have a reason for not dealing with something – just say 'Can I get back to you, I'm in the middle of something important/urgent?'

You have to learn to limit your availability, or you will never be able to manage your time – you will be constantly stopping what you are doing to deal with interruptions.

Limiting duration
Some of the things we do take a great deal of time for very little result. Later on we will look at Pareto's Principle, also called the 80/20 rule. This says that we spend approximately 80 per cent of our time doing work that produces only 20 per cent of the result. Unless these jobs are important, there is little point in spending a lot of time on something that really isn't worth it. Set sensible limits on how long you will spend on a job, and if it takes longer than you can afford, evaluate whether you really need to finish it, considering all the other things you have to get done. Most people get a sense of accomplishment from completing things, but using your time to feed your sense of accomplishment isn't a very good use of it!

Limiting importance
Not everything is important. Even if it were, there would be degrees of importance – not everything can have equal priority. Check that you aren't over-emphasising the importance of some tasks. Do you, for example, treat all work for a particular person as important? Do

you check how important something is when you receive work? Or do you just assume? You can't do everything, so spend most of your time on the most important work, and if you have to skimp on time, skimp on things that *aren't* important.

Limiting involvement

However much we may mean well, it is easy to become overcommitted. We need to limit our involvement in things, so we work only on things that we **should** be using our time on. Most of us like being involved – it's nice to have a finger in lots of pies, to feel necessary and needed, even important. But it can also take up too much of our valuable time.

Delegation is an important time management skill. It means stepping back from personally handling things to delegate them to others. You are still involved, but to a limited extent, saving you time.

Limiting standards

For most things we do, there is an acceptable standard. If there isn't, we usually mentally set one for ourselves, and often without ever realising we are doing it. But are we setting sensible standards? Perfectionists like everything to be perfect – their standard is perfection. But even if we aren't perfectionists, we often set artificially high standards. You can save a great deal of time by doing things **well enough**. Doing them better than necessary is a waste of time. Try to adjust your mental standards to do things appropriately, rather than working to ideals that cost you time which could be better spent on other things.

Limiting urgency

Not everything needs doing today. We all know that, and I'm sure you can all think of a number of things that don't have to be done straight away. These are things we **plan** to do at a later time/date. But often we over-emphasise a task's urgency, like its importance. We feel we must do things **now**, and that they can't wait. Urgency determines **when** you do things: in what order. So giving priority to things that are non-urgent leaves you rushed to deal with the really urgent matters.

Changing your thinking

Figure 1 shows how you may need to change your ways of thinking in order to set appropriate limits and improve your time management.

	Wrong thinking	Right thinking
Limiting availability	I have to stop what I'm doing to answer the phone/speak to...	Is this interruption *really* more important than what I'm doing right now? If it is, fair enough. If not, it can wait!
Limiting duration	I've started so I might as well finish.	Just because you've started something, it doesn't mean you have to persevere to the bitter end, especially if something more important or urgent comes along. It's OK to give up and get on with things you *can* finish.
Limiting importance	It's all important.	No it isn't! Sort out your priorities and plan your time accordingly.
Limiting involvement	If you want a job doing, you'd better do it yourself.	You can't do it all. Only get involved in things that need *you* to do them, and let others take care of the rest.
Limiting standards	If a job's worth doing, it's worth doing well.	A job's only worth doing *well enough* – it doesn't have to be perfect.
Limiting urgency	This can't wait.	Or can it? What would happen if I wasn't here to do this? Is it the *most* urgent thing you need to do? Is it really the best use of your time *right now*?

Fig. 1. Setting limits.

QUESTIONS AND ANSWERS

Surely if I start saying I can't do something because I'm too busy, people will think I can't cope with my job. That's not going to help my career much, is it?

Being competent and capable is one thing – but you're not a superhero! Would you rather say nothing and then let someone down when you can't keep up with all the requests for your time? Speaking up when you're becoming overloaded lets people know how little time you have available. It enables *them* to prioritise the work they are giving you, so they use your time effectively.

I don't like to compromise the standard of my work. Surely it's better to do a good job and produce quality work than do rushed jobs that aren't properly finished?

Most people gain a sense of satisfaction from doing good quality work: a job well done makes us feel proud. But most people's jobs aren't necessarily measured by purely quality – they also depend on **quantity**. Checking standards enables you to focus on doing important jobs to a high standard, and not compromising your standards of quality. You can gain yourself the time to do this by processing non-important jobs quickly and easily, to a reduced standard because they simply aren't worth the time and effort to put more work into them. It doesn't all have to be perfect.

DECIDING WHAT TO DO WITH YOUR TIME

So, what should you do with your time? It's surprising how few people know the answer to this at work. What are you actually there for? What's the purpose of your job? You can't be more effective unless you know what you're trying to achieve!

Spend time doing the right things

The principles of time management are simple: you need to spend your time on actually doing things, not being busy. Anyone can be busy, but you need to be busy **on the right things**. Chapter 3 will help you with this. Some people just get stuck into their work every day, and beaver away with little planning or discrimination as to what they will do and in what order. Hence, they can sometimes spend as much time doing minor, irrelevant things as they do on important tasks. Planning and prioritising will help you focus your effort appropriately.

Spend time doing what you like doing

In an ideal world, you could decide what to spend your time on based on choice: doing the things you enjoy doing. But for most of us, this is a dream rather than reality. But, if we *could* focus on improving the amount of time we spend on tasks we actually enjoy, and limiting the time spent on tasks we don't, most of us would be happier. And when we feel happier, we usually get more done: we achieve more.

Spend time doing what you're good at

Do you know what your strengths and weaknesses are? If you do, you can decide what things you're good at, and try to work accordingly. Work you can do easily can be done in difficult times – for example, first thing in the morning, or when you're pushed for time. Tasks that you find difficult will need more concentration and effort, so plan these in so they aren't rushed, or handled when you're not at your best.

Spend time on results, not effort

As we said earlier, you need to spend your time on achieving things, not being busy. Achievement makes most people feel good, so they are motivated and will work better. A commonly quoted rule is the 80/20 rule, or Pareto's Principle. This states that typically 80 per cent of effort achieves only 20 per cent of results. Thus, 80 per cent of the results are achieved from only 20 per cent of your working effort. (See Figure 2.)

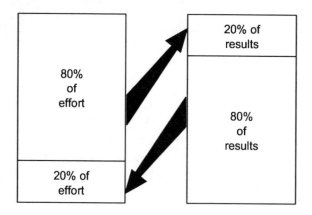

Fig. 2. The 80/20 rule.

But what does this actually mean? Well, put simply, most of the time we spend is wasted – it produces very little result. If we could focus on the aspects of our work that yield most results, we would be enormously more productive.

Spend time at the right time
Most of us have some awareness of our personal body clock: most people realise that they work better at certain times than at others. You need to be aware of this, and work appropriately. If you can identify which aspects of your work produce the most results, then do these when you are at your best. Put simply, people's energy levels and blood sugar fluctuates throughout the day, and so eating and drinking can affect how you work. If you start to become tired and can't concentrate, it may be because you have low blood sugar. Plan your day around your most productive times.

SETTING GOALS

Setting goals is something that surprisingly few people do. No wonder that so few of us achieve what we want.

Why set goals?
- Goals can increase your motivation.

- Goals can raise your self-confidence when you achieve them.

- Goals help you achieve more.

- Goals help you decide what to do with your time.

- Goals improve your performance.

- Goals increase your personal satisfaction when you achieve them.

- Goals tend to improve your concentration.

- People who set goals tend to suffer less from stress and/or anxiety.

Setting goals properly
As with most things in life, there is a right and a wrong way to set goals. Later on, this book will show you how to write **objectives**. 'Objectives' is simply another word for goals. You will see how to set **SMART** objectives. SMART is a way of jogging your memory to always write good objectives/goals. For now, you should understand the principles of goal-setting correctly.

Set positive goals
Phrase goals positively.

e.g. 'Deal with John Briggs more effectively – be more assertive...'
not 'Don't give in to John Briggs so often.'

Set specific goals
You can't tell if you have achieved something unless you can measure your success. Be precise. Give dates, times, amounts, numbers, rather than woolly goals. If you don't make goals precise, it's hard to tell whether you've achieved them or not, and you can lull yourself into a false sense of security when you are actually not making much progress.

e.g. 'Reduce cigarette smoking to eight per day.'
not 'Cut down on smoking.'

Set realistic goals
Your goals are *your* goals. It's all too easy to set goals based on other people's expectations, rather than our own. Also, we tend to base goals on our ideal – our best performance, regardless of whenever that actually happened. For example, if you went swimming and swam 20 lengths one day, when you were feeling particularly relaxed and 'in the mood', it would be easy to set a goal to swim 20 lengths every time you go swimming. But would you either want to or be able to do that? Set goals based realistically on what you can achieve, without being too optimistic. The benefits of achieving goals will be denied you, if you don't achieve them because they are too hard or unrealistic. This can be demotivating. Set goals you can achieve.

e.g. 'Exercise a minimum of one hour a week until June, then increase to two hours per week.'
not 'Exercise a minimum of two hours per week.'

Set goals at the right level
By the same token, don't make your goals too easy! People can do this because they are afraid of failure, and so don't like to risk not achieving a goal. Also, it's a by-product of laziness. You need to set goals so that they do stretch you a little – otherwise there's no point in having them!

Set goals for performance, not outcome
If you set goals based on outcomes, you lose control of your ability to achieve them. For example, setting a goal such as winning a race is dependent on *other runners'* performances, as well as your own. Such a goal is **outcome-dependent**. Instead, set goals based on *your own* performance, such as 'run the race in a personal best time'. Over a period of time, the motivation and sense of reward and achievement you will feel from achieving goals will reduce if you use outcome goals rather than performance ones. Outcome goals are dependent on other people, or circumstances that we can't always control. Competition only motivates us if it's there. As soon as the competition becomes too strong for us to cope with, or so weak that we aren't challenged by it, it stops motivating us.

e.g. 'Increase number of new business contacts opened by 20 per cent.'
not 'Open more new business contacts than anyone else.'

Keep goals small
Keep goals at a manageable level. For example, to buy a new car may be a large goal: so large that you don't have a clue how to go about it! Break large goals down into small ones so that you can achieve them and see what you have to do easily.

e.g. 'Pay off existing car loan.'
     'Save £500 deposit.'
     'Get car repaired to improve its selling price.'
     'Buy new car.'
not 'Buy a new car.'

Write goals down
Once you've decided on your goals, write them down. You probably think you know them, but there's no substitute for a list on a piece of paper, so you can see things being ticked off as you achieve them. It gives us a sense of accomplishment, and motivates us to do more.

Give goals priorities
Once you have written down your goals, one last step: give them priorities. Decide what to do first and number your goals accordingly. This enables you to focus your time and attention appropriately.

Personal goal-setting

People often get trapped into having good practices at work, but not applying them to their personal lives. This means that they can be efficient and organised at work, but still not satisfied and achieving what they want from life at home. Don't neglect setting yourself personal goals.

Personal goals *are* important, as we can all too easily end up not achieving what we want with our lives. Take time to write down your personal goals. This isn't a 'wish-list' full of daydreams, but a precise list of what in life is important to you. Consider all the things you want to do with your life. List them as goals. This will give you a means of prioritising and achievement *outside* work, as well as in your job. Here are some ideas for personal goals, but you will need to make your own list. Note that these are simply *ideas*, and have not been written properly as goals, as discussed above.

Creative goals
- Decorate the house.

- Landscape the garden.

- Learn to tango.

- Take a painting class.

- Write a novel.

Career goals
- Become a manager or supervisor.

- Gain a pay rise.

- Move into a role with more travel.

- Retire early.

- Work part-time.

Education goals
- Do an evening class.

- Gain an extra qualification.

- Learn a language.

- Learn to use the Internet.

- Read more non-fiction books.

Family goals
- Get married.

- Spend more time with the children.

- Start a family.

- Visit my parents more often.

Financial goals
- Build up a pension fund.

- Save at least £x.xx every month.

- Reduce mortgage payments.

- Repay debts and credit cards.

- Retire early.

Mental goals
- Accept my faults and work on my good points.

- Be more sociable.

- Control my temper more.

- Stop procrastinating.

- Stop criticising.

Physical goals
- Cut down on junk food.

- Cycle to work once a week.

- Lose weight.

- Reduce tea and coffee intake.

- Run a half marathon.

- Stop smoking.

- Take an exercise class once a week.

Social/pleasure goals
- Go to the cinema once a month.

- Have friends round once a month.

- Read more.

- Start a new hobby.
- Take a long weekend twice a year and go away.
- Take an evening class.

CHECKLIST

- Be aware of your own limits.
- Do things well enough – don't set unnecessarily high standards, or aim for perfection.
- Set proper goals.
- Your personal life shouldn't be forgotten – set goals for this also.

CASE STUDIES

Harassed Harriet

Harriet is a manager. She is in her early thirties, and revels in being well thought of at work. Just as well, because she spends most of her time there! She always has a stack of incoming mail to deal with, and when she eventually gets round to going through it, often finds it is simply too late to do what was required. Therefore, she does a lot of delegating to her colleagues, who are less busy and more able to meet the short deadlines that seem to be a fact of Harriet's life. She can't always spare the time to brief them, as she spends most of her time either in meetings, or on the way to them. She always seems to come back with more work, arising from these meetings, but never seems to get time to do it all. She works hard – the problem isn't that she doesn't get the work done. There's just so much of it, and it's all equally important. She usually comes home late, stressed and tired, and sure in the knowledge that her over-stuffed diary for tomorrow holds even more of the same.

Laid-back Larry

Larry is Harriet's husband, and in this case, opposites *must* have attracted! Larry is an author, and works from home, specialising in business and academic books. No matter how Harriet tries to get him organised, he always seems to work at one pace – and it's not the same as Harriet's. He does the majority of the cooking and shopping, and is usually relaxing with a good book by the time his wife comes home in the evenings. He has deadlines to work to, and never seems to have any trouble renegotiating them – fortunately! He has plenty of time to get all his work done, so Harriet simply can't understand why he always seems to have so much left to do – or why this doesn't bother him. He has a nasty panic sometimes, when the deadline for a book is due, mainly because he always piles up work until the last minute.

Sympathetic Susan

Susan is Harriet's colleague. They have different work to do, but Harriet is more senior, and so does a great deal of delegating. Susan plans well, and manages her time so that she can spend plenty of it at home in the evenings, riding her two horses. So when last-minute panics happen, she is upset by the inconvenience, and it can cost her money, if she has to make last-minute alternative arrangements to look after the animals. She has good systems for her work, and always knows where everything can be found – unless Harriet has been rummaging for something to take to another urgent meeting! Susan's work systems would work well without all the interruptions – either work from Harriet, or people telephoning for her. In fact, taking messages for Harriet is Susan's main interruption, and she is beginning to find all the disruption frustrating.

DISCUSSION POINTS

1. Write a list of goals to assist you in work over the next month. Word these carefully, so the goals are set properly.

2. Consider your personal goals, and make a list of these. Do any of them conflict with work goals? If so, which is the more important to you? Adjust both lists if necessary, so your work and personal goals are compatible.

3. Look through the section on 'Setting limits'. Do you relate to any of the headings particularly? If so, how is this affecting your work? Think of specific examples when you have thought like this, and try to see how a different attitude would have affected your working.

2
Finding the Barriers to Time Management

Time management is often something that we *make* difficult. We have barriers to doing things – some mental, some physical. Some barriers we can remove or change, but others we can't. If we can't change things to suit ourselves, then we need to be aware of the barriers and try to find ways of working round them. There are three main barriers to good time management:

- mental
- physical
- people.

Each of these will have the effect of reducing your ability to successfully manage your time, if you do not recognise them, and either remove or work round them where possible.

REALISING YOUR MENTAL BARRIERS

Most of us have mental barriers. These arise, causing us to do things the way we do because:

- we believe it's right to do them that way
- we believe we can't do them another way
- we believe it's best to do them that way
- we've just never considered changing the way we do them

and so on – the list is practically endless.

There are many mental barriers to good time management, but we are going to concentrate on:

- control
- procrastination

- immediacy

- insecurity.

Control

The biggest mental barrier is believing that other people and circumstances control our time. This is partly true, but there is an awful lot (and probably more than you realise) which you can do to keep control of your own time. Try not to be manipulated by people and/or events. If you don't take control of your own time and schedule, you'll never manage your time successfully.

Problems with control

Controlling your schedule and time *too* rigidly can mean that you aren't flexible. You won't be available to deal with emergencies. Imagine working with someone who schedules in every minute of every day. Where's the time for unplanned, important events that need their attention? What if you need to talk to them about something? If you over-control your time, you may well leave others feeling frustrated because they can't access you or your time – you're never available, and sometimes people can't deal with things while you're out, and they can't find out *when* you will be free.

On the other hand, letting others control your time can cause nearly as many difficulties as it solves! If other people have open access to your diary, you lose control of what *you* want to do, and end up doing what others want you to do. You may eventually end up feeling powerless and depressed as you are controlled, like a puppet, by others.

Avoiding or overcoming control difficulties

- Don't allow others unrestricted access to your diary – unless you can trust them with it.

- Don't make yourself unavailable for others. They need your help to do their work, and manage their own time.

- Don't over-schedule – you will run out of time for dealing with unscheduled crises and emergencies.

- You need to strike a balance between controlling your own time, and letting others help you.

Procrastination

Procrastination is putting off something or things that should be done – intentionally. Delays and postponements will always be part of life, but when you procrastinate, you **deliberately** put off things which you ought to be doing. Procrastination can be such a problem that it is dealt with in much more detail later in this book.

Problems with procrastination

A little procrastination isn't too bad – but what it *does* do is store up trouble. What you didn't do today will still be there tomorrow. And tomorrow... and tomorrow... and so on. The word 'procrastinate' actually comes from the Latin word for 'tomorrow'. Things won't disappear just because you forget about them.

Eventually, you will end up with too much to do in one day, and so something will be missed. Also, starting every day with a large number of tasks which have been left from previous days is daunting. It may weigh you down, and when you feel under pressure or stress, you may not be able to perform at your best. Finally, the sense of failure when you see things that *haven't* been achieved isn't a good thing. It's demotivating. By contrast, the sense of achievement when you see the things you *have* achieved, *is* motivating. And when you feel good, generally speaking, you work better.

Avoiding or overcoming procrastination
- Practise **delayed gratification**. This means getting on with work and getting things done now, so you don't have to do them later. That way, when tomorrow comes, you can experience all the freedom and free time you didn't have today. Unfortunately, it's not easy for a lot of people.

- **Question your motives**. Ask yourself *why* you are procrastinating. So you can do something more enjoyable? More interesting? Less difficult? Because you don't *want* to do it, so are delaying the inevitable? Ask *why* you are procrastinating, and you may find the answer as to how to stop doing it. Procrastination tends to have a common theme.

- Try mentally thinking of it as **investing time**, rather than delayed gratification. Delayed gratification often seems negative – it's *not* doing what you want to now. 'Investing time' sounds and feels more positive – it's doing things now so that you can do what you want later. Do today what you *don't* want to do, so you can do tomorrow what you *do* want to do: invest time to make time, remember?

- Try to avoid procrastinating as much as possible. Do things **now** whenever you can. I don't mean letting yourself get interrupted all the time, but try to get as many things as possible done and out of the way.

Immediacy

The opposite of procrastination is immediacy – wanting to do everything now and not wait – not being able to bear the thought of leaving things for tomorrow. Think of it as 'hurry sickness' – not regulating what you do. It's often the reason why so many people work such long hours.

Problems with immediacy

The problem with immediacy is that it's often self-defeating. Working longer and longer to do more and more means we get tired. And when we get tired, we make more mistakes, and we work slower. So like a hamster on a wheel going nowhere, we carry on working away, achieving less and less, to a lower and lower standard.

Avoiding or overcoming immediacy

- Basically, slow down, and pace yourself.

- Bite off the work in manageable mouthfuls, leaving what you can't manage for a snack later.

- Check how urgent things really are. Just because someone wants something, it doesn't mean they need it today. Always ask **when** things are required – establish the deadline.

- Remember, there's another day tomorrow. And another week next week.

Insecurity

Insecurity is based on fear: fear of losing things, fear of not being able to find things, fear of all sorts of things. Even fear of not looking busy. A cluttered desk doesn't make you look efficient and busy. It makes you look disorganised, and inefficient. You will need to conquer insecurity to do many of the time management techniques you will find in this book.

Problems with insecurity

Insecurity makes you feel uneasy. Just feeling uneasy can make your work suffer: stress inhibits certain brain functions. In any event, fear isn't a good reason for working in a certain way. Fear of losing or not being able to find things can lead to us retaining mountains of paper in complex filing systems that are little used. Fear of not looking busy can lead us to keep paperwork which isn't necessary on our desks and workspace. But all these things only get in the way of what we really need to do – get on with our work.

Avoiding or overcoming insecurity

• Be more concerned with *what* you achieve than *how* you achieve it.

• Decide whether you should keep something based on whether it has enough value to you and your work to warrant the time, energy and cost of saving it.

• Don't be afraid to throw things away or pass them on.

• Don't keep the things you *want*, keep the things you *need*.

• Don't retain things just because they are interesting.

• Try to work efficiently, however it may look to others.

UNDERSTANDING PEOPLE BARRIERS

For many years, psychologists have described two types of behaviour that people exhibit: they call these Type A and Type B. Type A people are driving, ambitious 'do-ers', who don't like delays and waiting. Type B people are more calm and easy-going, and often work more thoroughly and with attention to detail. Type A people tend to focus on quantity – time, achievement, progress. Type B people, on the other hand, tend to focus more on quality – standards, perfection, details, a job well done.

The extent to which you exhibit Type A or B behaviour will determine how you work, and your attitude to time management. But rather than concentrate on personality-type tests to determine the extent of your Type A or B behaviour, let's look at some common people problems behind time management. I suspect that most people will be able to recognise someone they know in the following pages.

The optimist

Positive thinking is a good thing. But I'm sure we all know people with good intentions, who like to believe they can move mountains. Being too optimistic is being unrealistic. These people can let you down. They commit to things and then can't achieve them. This sort of problem requires the simple ability to say 'no'. It may be simple, but it isn't always easy, which is why people fall into this trap. Optimists are good starters of work, but poor finishers.

Improving optimists
- Be realistic.

- Don't let rosy thoughts take over your common sense.

- Don't take on more than you know you can achieve.

- If you aren't sure, say so, don't just commit to something.

- Keep some time back for emergencies.

- Schedule finish times, or **deadlines** for tasks, not just start times.

The perfectionist

Perfectionists set impossibly high standards, and then set about achieving them. The problem with this is that there is always more that could be done: more information to be obtained, more ideas to think of, more people to consult or to discuss with, and so on. The trouble is that perfectionists often take so long to do something that its value is reduced. Perfectionists are also good starters, but poor finishers.

Improving perfectionists
- Do things well enough.

- Don't focus on quality at the expense of quantity.

- Don't miss deadlines to do work to a better standard.

- Don't set standards above those of the people you are carrying out the task for – unless you really can afford the time.

- Schedule deadlines or finish times for tasks, to make sure you don't lose sight of the end of the task in the detail.

The rebel

Rebels are like defiant children. They are at pains to be in control of others and their environment. These people often set their own deadlines, with no reference to others, or no consideration of others' timescales and requirements. These people relish crises and problems, as they can overcome these to show how much in control they really are. Rebels are good finishers, but poor starters of work.

Improving rebels

● Don't inconvenience others: work to accommodate their requirements.

● Don't leave things to the last minute simply to feel more important: it's risky.

● Get started on jobs, as getting started is often a rebel's weak area.

● Try to take account of other people's needs.

● You don't have to prove yourself all the time. It's all right to fail once in a while.

The socialite

These people like to be involved with people. They like to talk, discuss, know what's going on, gather information. They can be both easily distracted and distracting to others. They can get easily caught up in trivia, at the expense of important work. Open-plan offices are wonderful for these people – they can hear and join in everything. But they can be a source of endless distraction and interruption to others.

Improving socialites

● Don't distract others: start conversations with 'Do you have a minute?', and *accept it* if people say 'no'.

● Don't take rejection personally: it just means that people are busy, not that they don't like you or don't *want* to talk to you.

● Try to keep socialising down to the level required for a good working relationship.

● You don't have to be involved in everything.

The worrier

Some people never seem to develop confidence in their own ability. These people may avoid certain types of work, because they worry they will be unable to do it, which will further damage their self-esteem. Often, these people are prone to procrastination: putting things off because they are afraid to try them in case they fail.

Improving worriers
- Ask for help when you need it.

- Don't bite off more than you can chew, but don't be afraid to stretch yourself, either.

- Get someone else to check over your work for errors. This can boost your confidence. You could have an arrangement with a friend or colleague that you check each other.

- Negotiate unpressured deadlines, so you can carry out work you're concerned about with no time pressure.

- Talk things over with your boss, if you can. Explain your concerns, and ask for some assistance.

QUESTIONS AND ANSWERS

Surely if it's in my nature to worry, or to be a bit of a perfectionist, I can't do a great deal about it?

Yes you can. Children aren't *born* worriers, or perfectionists – they learn those behaviours by the way they are brought up, because of their experiences, and because they find it suits them in some way. These things, which were learned in the first place, can be **unlearned**. You will experience far more calm and relief if you can stop being driven to behave in this way.

I work with someone who seems to exhibit several of these behaviours and she seems to have mental barriers as well. What can I do about that?

Try to work on one thing at a time. Choose one behaviour you want to work on, or to learn to deal with, and adapt accordingly. When you are finding her easier to deal with on that issue, you can choose another thing. Take things one at a time – and always remember, you can't change other people, you can only change yourself, and hope that that helps you to cope with them, or that they change in response.

GETTING STARTED

Before you can start good time management, you need to know what needs to be improved. You need a base to start from. Almost every book on time management will tell you to start off by making a **time log**: by recording what you currently spend your time on. And because this itself takes time and effort, it's something that often puts people off time management altogether! You need to understand *why* making a log is so very important, to give you an incentive to do it.

Imagine you're going on a journey, and you need to know how to get there. Unless you know where you are at the moment, you can't look up directions on a map, or work out how to get where you're going. If you want to be better at time management, you need to know where you're starting from. It would be silly to spend your valuable time reading a book on time management that told you only 20 per cent of what you need to know, but advised 80 per cent of what you're doing already!

So, you need to establish where you're starting from, so you know what improvements you need to make. Whilst time management books usually advocate a full time log, don't spend so much of your time doing this that it becomes a problem in its own right!

Recording how you spend your time

Keep a note in a notebook or somewhere similar, of what you do throughout your working day. Note down **everything** – including all the little things like trips to the toilet, cups of coffee, sitting and taking a breather, even chatting: the whole truth.

Here are some useful categories. They are just pointers to get you started – make up your own as you go along, so you have everything you spend your time on categorised:

- appointments
- chatting
- coffee
- collecting printing from the printer
- daydreaming
- dealing with interruptions
- eating
- e-mailing
- faxing
- meetings

- opening mail
- photocopying
- prioritising
- reading
- reviewing proposals
- supervising others
- telephone calls – incoming
- telephone calls – outgoing
- thinking
- toilet
- travelling
- writing correspondence
- writing proposals.

At the end of a reasonable period of time (I usually say at least ten days, which for most people equates to two working weeks), do some quick sums and tot up what you've spent your time on.

So what do you do with the results? Well, the first thing is that you'll probably be surprised by them! Without some concrete facts to go on it's hard to estimate just what we spend our time on – so most people find the answer a surprise. What you need to do, is to ask yourself some general questions, and be **honest** about the results.

- At what time of the day did I get the most done? At what time of day did I get the least achieved? This will tell you when you are most productive.

- How much time do I spend on avoidable inefficiency: waiting, looking for things, being interrupted, etc.? This will give you areas that you can work on, because if you can reduce or even eliminate these, there will be a substantial time saving.

- How much time did I spend on unnecessary tasks? This will give you ammunition to question whether you need to do these things, and if you do, *why* you need to do them, if they are so time-consuming.

- How much time did I spend on tasks that I could or should have got someone else to do? This will indicate whether you should delegate more.

- Did I achieve all the things I should have done? If not, why not?

This will give you pointers for immediate improvement.

CHECKLIST

- Accept that you can't do everything – so stop trying.
- Don't be so optimistic you overcommit yourself.
- Don't procrastinate – do things straight away, or at least with a minimum of delay.
- Keep socialising to the level required for good working relationships.
- Make a time log – and learn from it.
- Strike a balance between controlling your time, and being available for others.

CASE STUDIES

Harriet is obviously harassed

Harriet seems to think she's Superwoman! Susan listens to her on the telephone all the time she's in the office (which admittedly isn't often), taking calls, and adding yet more meetings and appointments into her diary. She knows that all that will happen eventually is that Harriet will have to let people down, cancelling low priority meetings to attend important or urgent ones.

'Harriet, why don't you say you can't do some of these meetings now, rather than saying yes to them all and dropping out nearer the time?' Susan asked. 'Well, I'm hoping that things will have eased off by then,' Harriet replied. Both of the women looked sceptically at Harriet's in-tray. How on earth could things ease off when Harriet was too busy in meetings to clear her workload?

Harriet needs to learn to accept that she can't do everything. Letting people down now by saying 'no' is better than letting them down at the last minute by being too busy and preoccupied to deal with them with the care and attention they want. The real truth is, Harriet *likes* to be busy. It makes her feel important.

Larry is the secret rebel

Larry is usually waiting at home for Harriet, with some dinner prepared. She often lets off steam about her job and all the pressure she's under. He doesn't seem to have a care in the world, and shrugs off stress as something that happens to other people. Really, he's a rebel. He always leaves everything to the last minute, and then pulls all the stops out to achieve things just in time. In fact, the 'Just In Time' management technique might have been named Larry's Rule!

When Harriet has deadlines at home, such as delivery dates for furniture, or she needs to book their holiday, Larry's attitude infuriates her. He doesn't seem to be able to commit himself to anything. It's as if he doesn't use a diary at all. In fact, he makes himself feel important by being difficult. His laid-back attitude is a mask for his rebellion against being organised, scheduled, told what to do.

Susan is secretly scared

On the surface, Susan is well-organised and efficient. She doesn't get overcommitted, and never seems to fail to deliver – the perfect complement in a lot of ways to harassed Harriet. But Susan can be just as inefficient. She has never done a time log, as she is nervous about what it would reveal. In fact, she's often nervous, but she covers it well by being organised and in control.

She could do a lot to help herself *and* Harriet, if only she would speak up more often when Harriet is being silly. But she doesn't want to be seen to be disloyal. Also, she is secretly nervous that Harriet might get angry with her – after all, Harriet is more senior than her.

One of the main reasons, in fact, why she gets so much done and holds things together so well for Harriet is that she doesn't want to be seen to be struggling. It would make her look a failure, after all – wouldn't it?

DISCUSSION POINTS

1. Assess what mental barriers to time management you have, if any. How can you overcome these to start working in a better way?

2. Make a time log for at least ten working days. Analyse it, and see exactly where all your time goes.

3. Try making a time log for your home time as well. Can you improve how you spend your time at home – to make it not necessarily more efficient, but simply more enjoyable?

3
Effective and Efficient Prioritising

Good time management rests on two things: effectiveness and efficiency. Both are important to managing your time well, but few people actually understand the difference. Instead, we tend to use the terms interchangeably, as if they mean the same thing – but they don't. You need to understand the difference between the two.

Effectiveness means being productive, being capable of achieving. In time management terms, it's about **doing the right things**. Efficiency means functioning effectively with the least waste of effort. In time management terms, it's about **doing things in the right way**. Figure 3 shows a way of looking at your time in terms of effectiveness and efficiency.

	EFFECTIVE	NOT EFFECTIVE
EFFICIENT	• Doing the right things in the right way • Doing the right things well	• Doing the wrong things well
NOT EFFICIENT	• Doing the right things in the wrong way • Doing the right things badly	• Doing the wrong things badly

Fig. 3. Effectiveness v. efficiency.

Doing the right things well
High effectiveness plus high efficiency. This means finding out what you should be doing, and doing it in a way that optimises the outcomes. You need to know what needs doing, and how best to do

it – a pretty reasonable definition of someone who's good at their job, in many ways!

Doing the wrong things well

Low effectiveness, but high efficiency. Everyone likes to do things well. But remember the 80/20 rule – doing well things that don't matter to your job won't help you, or anyone else. Very often, the recognition and success that people achieve at work comes from doing the right things well – and being seen to be doing a good job at them. Many people complain that they don't get noticed, although they do good work. This is often because their work is excellent, but not the sort of work that is important, and so it goes unnoticed.

Doing the right things badly

High effectiveness, but low efficiency. This is where people do the right things, and focus their efforts on what is important, but do them badly. Everyone needs practice, but in this instance, maybe these jobs would be better handled by someone capable of doing them better.

Doing the wrong things badly

Low effectiveness plus low efficiency. Sometimes we come across people like this. They don't seem to be able to get anything right! No wonder they do the wrong things – it often happens that they get given low grade work because they make so many mistakes, and can't be trusted with more important tasks. People who work like this are sure to make an impression – but not a positive one. These people don't have their priorities right, and what they do handle, they handle badly.

UNDERSTANDING EFFECTIVENESS

As we have said above, effectiveness is about **doing the right things**. It's about deciding what you're going to do, and more importantly, what you aren't. You need to look at effectiveness in this way. Then afterwards, you can do the things you *are* going to do, **efficiently**.

Consider your time log – the one you were asked to do in Chapter 2. If you didn't make one, you really should give this a try. If you really can't face it, however, just make a list of all the things you do during a working day – and that includes going to the toilet, making cups of coffee, chatting – **everything**.

Now, let's take a close look at the list or time log. You should have here, in one form or another, a complete list of what you do. It should include tasks that are half-completed, routine jobs, non-work items, time-wasting things, all sorts! What you need to do now is to go through it, and see how effective you are in carrying out your workload.

Delegating

Any activities which **shouldn't** be done by you, mark with a 'D' for 'delegate'. These are the tasks that are taking up your time unnecessarily. Also, mark up any tasks which **could** be done by others, even if they are logically part of your own work. The idea is that, over a period of time, you will work towards delegating some of these as well, or at the very least, you can delegate them at peak times when you get really busy, in order to create some extra time for yourself.

Delegation will be covered in full later in this book, but try to be open-minded at this stage. Don't refrain from putting a 'D' next to something just because you **like** doing it, or **want** to do it. The plan isn't to deprive you of all the things you enjoy, but to identify those you **could** remove if you needed to.

Pruning

The next step is to look for the tasks that shouldn't be done at all – by anyone. These can be pruned from your list. It's surprising how many things we do that might turn out to be unnecessary, if we went and asked the other people involved with the task. No one is saying you can suddenly stop doing these things: you'll have to talk to others, and establish if the tasks really are as superfluous as they seem. Over a period of time, however, most people are able to at least reduce some of these tasks.

This may sound unlikely to you, but it's surprising how often people do things because, historically, they always have. Very often, when the need for something reduces, people don't think to tell you to stop doing it. But if you ask them, they may be happy for you to stop doing some of these tasks.

Prioritising

Now you are left with the tasks that **you should do**. Doing these should mean you're effective – you're doing the right things. Now you need to be efficient – to do them in the best way. This is where prioritising, planning and the other areas in this book come in.

UNDERSTANDING EFFICIENCY

Efficiency means functioning effectively with the least waste of effort. In time management terms, it's about **doing things in the right way**. The whole of this book is about efficiency really: good time management is one of the best ways to be efficient.

To be efficient, you need to plan your time and tasks wisely, and to plan, you need to prioritise. In time management, everything sometimes seems to be interrelated.

USING EFFECTIVENESS AND EFFICIENCY

If you have concentrated first on effectiveness, you should have identified tasks that you will work towards eliminating – either by delegating them to others, or by stopping doing them altogether. The next step would be to prioritise. Basically, you just need to ask one or two questions:

- Is this task essential to my job, objectives or organisation?

- Is this task necessary but not absolutely essential?

This is all you need to do to identify high and low priority work. You have lots of categories of tasks now, but what you really need to establish is: 'What's the best use of my time right now?' Faced with a workload, what should you do first? To assess this, you will need to move on and consider relative importance and urgency.

QUESTIONS AND ANSWERS

I like to leave things until nearer the time when they're due – I find I get my best work done when it's near a deadline – it seems to sharpen my concentration. Are you saying I should stop this? After all, it's worked until now.

Focused working just before an impending deadline is something most people have experienced at some time or other. Very often, it produces good results. But it isn't a technique that you should rely on for a number of reasons. Firstly, are you sure you really produce your best work in this way? How do you know that if you gave your full, unhurried attention to a task, it wouldn't be even better? Secondly, pressure may motivate us, and get the adrenaline going to stimulate a good job. But too much of it can result in stress, rather than just pressure. Stress isn't good for us, and can inhibit your brain function so your work standard declines. Finally, you aren't allowing any time for unforeseen events – other priorities, emergencies, the deadline being brought forward, things like that. It's just too risky to be a good technique to rely on.

All this prioritising in this way seems very analytical. Surely most of us just know our jobs well enough to know what we ought to do and in what order?

It's surprising what you can see when you take a step back and look at something from a distance, rather than just from close range. Yes, most people do know their roles at work, and know what needs doing. But that doesn't mean they are doing things in the best way. Consultants and/or time and motion experts have made a great deal of money over the years by doing just this – taking a fresh look at things and finding improvements. People get into habits – habits of doing things in a certain order, in a certain way – all sorts of things. Rarely does the job you are shown when you start work stay the same – it **evolves** over time. You just need to check now and then that it has actually evolved for the better, rather than for the worse.

UNDERSTANDING IMPORTANCE AND URGENCY

Like effectiveness and efficiency, we often confuse importance and urgency. If you were asked to decide what part of your workload to do first, most people would say the most important thing. But if you think about it, just because something's **important**, is it **urgent**? Does it have to be done **first**? Of course not. They are two different things.

Important things are important – it's as simple as that. It doesn't mean you have to drop everything and do them right away, it doesn't even mean you have to do them today, but it means you have to do them, and do them properly. For example, birthdays are important. But you don't rush out on the first of January and buy all your birthday cards and presents and send them off! You wait until the right time (you could call it the **deadline**, if you like), and *then* you send them off.

If you don't remember it's someone's birthday until the day before, however, that's a situation where it becomes **urgent**, rather than important. See the difference? The trouble is, we get so caught up in the business of work that we tend to treat everything as urgent. But we might actually be better off treating important things as if they were less urgent, as then they would get the time and attention they deserve, instead of being rushed.

Tackling urgent tasks

Urgent tasks can often be done in **batches**. A good example of this would be telephone calls, which can often be done far quicker if you do a whole batch of them at once. Letter-writing is another example. Handling quantities of similar tasks in a batch can make you more productive – you get into a rhythm for the task, and each one takes less time. Things become easier.

By and large, you need to get urgent tasks out of the way but not spend too long on them. You could say that urgent tasks aren't important – **unless you don't get them done in time**!

Tackling important tasks

Important tasks shouldn't be rushed. You need to understand the concept of **positive delay**.

Positive delay is *not* procrastination. It is a deliberate delay, designed to be useful and positive. In contrast to procrastination, where you put something off, with positive delay, you choose instead to do the task at a better time. There is a fine line between the two, so be very careful about your motives, when you opt for positive delay! Here are some good reasons for choosing positive delay:

- Interruptions are likely.

- You are concerned that other tasks are more important.

- You are too tired to deal well with an important task.

- You are upset or angry, so not thinking clearly.

- You don't have enough information to get started and do a good job yet.

- You have to be somewhere else before you will have finished the task, or before you will have had enough time to make meaningful progress.

- You have something urgent to do, so your concentration is hampered by worrying about getting that task out of the way.

ASSESSING IMPORTANCE AND URGENCY

You can see from Figure 4 that urgent and important tasks require different treatment. There are no hard and fast rules for what to do when. Simply use your common sense.

	URGENT	NOT URGENT
IMPORTANT	Important *and* urgent things should be done immediately, taking sufficient time to do them well.	Important things that are not urgent can wait until you have the time to do them properly.
NOT IMPORTANT	Urgent but not important things need doing quickly to get them done and out of the way. But spend as little time as possible on these tasks.	Things that aren't urgent or important can be left until the very last: even if they're the things you enjoy doing most!

Fig. 4. Importance v. urgency.

Important and urgent

These tasks need to be done quickly and well. This is your top priority work. However, often tasks end up in this category because they weren't done before – before they became urgent. This category should be reserved for your top priority work – so don't add to this category by delaying things until they end up here.

Important but not urgent

These tend to be those tasks that require a lot of attention. Don't be tempted to put these off until they fall into the category above – that's only creating additional pressure and stress for yourself. These tasks should be broken down into tasks or stages, and started on to get some of their work out of the way to reduce the overall size of the task left. Try to plan to do some of these tasks every day if you can – you will soon get them done if you divide up the effort like this.

Urgent but not important

These tasks mustn't take too much of your time, because if they do, you will end up with not enough time for your important work. If you have a lot of tasks in this category, assess how important they are by asking yourself 'What would happen if I simply didn't do this?' It's surprising that once you think about it, many of these tasks can be abandoned.

Not urgent or important

These are the tasks you must quite simply stop doing. Either negotiate stopping them altogether, or delegate them.

MAKING 'TO DO' LISTS

Most people use lists in some way or another, if only for remembering shopping! To Do lists are very simple, but they are also very powerful and effective as a tool. This is because they have two effects:

- Firstly, they get you organised: they make sure you don't forget what needs to be done.

- Secondly, they can greatly reduce the amount of stress and worry that you have, by literally taking things off your mind (and placing them on to paper).

Starting the list

Getting things off your mind
Simply write down all the things you have to do or to remember. It is sensible at first to just clear your mind by writing down absolutely everything. Then you can move on to categorise, etc. Some people use cards, or small squares of paper, or sticky notes to do this. This enables you to sort tasks and shuffle their order, without having to rewrite them.

Breaking up large tasks
Just as when we talked about goals we mentioned breaking big ones down so they are achievable, once you have your list, look for tasks that can be broken down into a number of smaller tasks. Break them down in this way, so you have a larger number of smaller, more manageable tasks to focus on. If you do this, you will be surprised how much easier it is to get tasks started. Very often we are put off starting a task if it is a large, difficult one. So by breaking tasks down, we can overcome this problem.

Prioritising the list

Next, prioritise the list, based on how important or urgent tasks are. Remember, you will need to re-prioritise regularly, as deadlines approach and non-urgent tasks become more urgent with time.

Rewriting the list

This may seem a nuisance, but discipline yourself to go through your list and rewrite it at least once a week. I usually do this whilst travelling, or waiting for people or meetings, or even during a meeting if I don't need to pay attention!

Re-prioritise your list when you rewrite it. You will gain a sense of security from knowing *exactly* what you have to do and how soon. You will also feel a sense of achievement as you see your list changing over time. Finally, if you keep crossing things off your list and never rewrite it, it ends up taking a lot of time just to see what's on there and judge what to do next, which defeats the whole point of using lists to help you with time management!

CHECKLIST

- Aim to be both effective and efficient for as much of your time as you can.

- Don't confuse importance and urgency.

- Don't procrastinate. Positive delay isn't the same thing at all.

- Take every opportunity to identify tasks for delegation, or tasks you can stop doing altogether.

CASE STUDIES

Harriet's letter misses the post

Harriet was just about to leave her office for a meeting when the phone rang. It was Mark, her boss, wanting a response to a matter raised by a solicitor. The response was overdue, and needed actioning urgently. The query was quite trivial really, but did require prompt action. Harriet sent Susan to the meeting in her place, and Susan spent a whole hour and a half in the meeting, totally unprepared and neither contributing nor needing to be there.

When Susan returned, Harriet was only just finishing the letter, and had missed the last post. 'The telephone kept ringing,' she said, 'it was absolutely hopeless.' Susan asked why she hadn't taken it off the hook. 'Because half of the calls were things I needed to do,' Harriet replied. It transpired that she had spent most of the time answering calls and then acting on them! She hadn't got the letter done in time purely because she had dealt with things based solely on how urgent they were, and ignoring importance – which is also why the letter hadn't been replied to in the first place.

If only she had considered the relative urgency and importance of tasks, she might have seen that getting the letter in the post was the most important and urgent task at that time. The other urgent tasks were just that – urgent – but they weren't important.

Larry's publisher refuses to extend a deadline

Larry likes to leave everything to the last minute. He says this works well, as he does his best work then – he is at his most prolific as a writer when he's up against a tight deadline. With a book deadline approaching, therefore, he started the work about two months before it was due, as usual. By the time the deadline was only two weeks away, he had 30 per cent of the book still to write. He telephoned his publisher.

'But it's only another two weeks!' he was insisting down the telephone when Harriet came home. 'What's two weeks – I've always been on time before, haven't I?' He put the phone down in a temper.

'What's the matter?' Harriet asked. His publisher had refused to extend the deadline. Larry, usually late, had forgotten that he had already negotiated a longer than usual deadline on this book, so he could get on and re-do the garden. This deadline had already been stretched as far as it could go, and the printers and proofreaders were already booked.

He could do it in time – just! It would mean nothing but work for two weeks, *and* working in the evenings and at weekends. If only he had worked harder earlier, instead of relying on extending the deadline. After all, if he'd known he couldn't extend it, he would have started earlier, then his evenings and weekends wouldn't be looking so bleak.

Susan sorts through Harriet's papers

Harriet was away at a conference all day one Friday. Susan had a great deal to do, but then one major task was cancelled, and she found she had some spare time. She sat down at Harriet's desk, and went through all her papers.

Firstly, she went through and sorted things into piles. She made one pile of things that were 'past time' – where the deadlines had been and gone and Harriet had missed them. She discarded all unimportant things in this pile, and retained the rest for Harriet to see what she had missed. Next, she sorted all the important tasks that would need quite a bit of work to make sure they were done properly. She tried to sort these into an order.

She sorted all the urgent but not important tasks, and took those to handle herself, where she could. The rest she put right on top of Harriet's chair, so she couldn't miss them or put any other papers on top of them! She added a note to them saying 'Do these first'. Finally, she sorted out all the things that were for reading but that needed no action at all, and the useless items that Harriet would have put in the bin.

After all this, she thought she was finished. Then it occurred to her that Harriet would soon rifle through the papers and disrupt them. So she made a series of lists and left them on Harriet's desk. Each list detailed what was in each pile, and what action was required.

When Harriet returned to the office, she was delighted. She could decide what to take to each meeting with her, and so she always had something to hand to work on. Of course, it didn't take her long to return her desk to the usual chaos, but it was nice while it lasted.

DISCUSSION POINTS

1. Make a list of things that you do. Your job description, if you have one, would be a good starting point. If you don't, make the list and this will give you a rough job description. Try to categorise the work you do by importance and urgency, to give you a sense of your whole job, and what you should be focusing on.

2. Operate a To Do list and rewrite it regularly. Try to find the best way of doing this for you – experiment with a computer list, manually, on a stack of cards. Evolve a system that works for you.

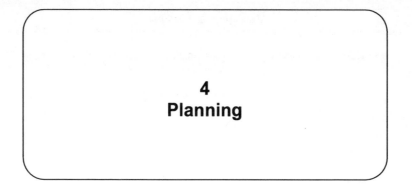

4
Planning

So, now we've learnt about efficiency and effectiveness, importance and urgency, we can get on and **do** things. Before you start **doing** anything, however, there's just one more thing we need to consider: planning. If you take a small amount of time to plan before you start anything, the way you do it will be most effective and/or efficient.

Planning means taking your To Do list, and your diary, and planning **what** you will do **when**. It's the step which most people leave out: they tend to think in vague terms: 'I'll do that later', 'that needs doing this week sometime', or 'I'll do that on Thursday afternoon'. But then things crowd in, and the time earmarked in the first place isn't available. This happens because the time hasn't been properly earmarked: it hasn't actually been planned and reserved for that particular task.

UNDERSTANDING PLANNING PROBLEMS

Here are just some of the biggest problems people experience with planning:

- Complex planning systems. These can take more time to plan than you need to do the work!

- Getting stuck into the work without taking time to plan first: perhaps meaning to plan, but getting carried away before you do.

- Lack of flexibility: making rigid plans that restrict you, and prevent flexibility in your work. This may make work inefficient, or just boring!

- Not setting objectives, so you don't know what really needs doing.

- Over-planning: not starting until everything is planned, or getting bogged down with every little detail instead of getting on with the work.

- Relying too heavily on experience. Knowing what you are doing doesn't mean you don't have to plan.

- Resisting change: planning often tends to make changes to the way you are used to doing things, so some people avoid planning just because of this.

- Setting woolly objectives, so you can't achieve them, or you can't tell when you have achieved them.

- Simply not bothering to plan.

- Spending more time planning than working!

KEEPING A DIARY

Most people have a diary in some shape or form. Consider how best to utilise one for work. Personal organisers have become increasingly popular in recent years, but these can cause as many problems as they cure, if you don't use them effectively. Whatever sort of diary you use, try to adopt broad principles that will make it work for you, to best advantage.

Most of us think of a diary as something essential for booking things in. Diaries will take care of the big things – birthdays, days off, holidays, training courses, meetings. What you really need to get **organised** and save yourself time by being efficient is a **schedule**.

Using electronic diaries

Electronic diaries can be useful. Whether or not you like technology, they do have certain advantages over normal, paper-based diary systems.

- They can be restricted – to not accept appointments at certain times, for example.

- They can prevent conflict – not accepting appointments which conflict with others already scheduled.

- They can remind you of appointments, by beeping or sending you an on-screen message.

- You can cross-reference tasks and appointments in them, creating links to other entries far more easily than with a paper-based diary.

- You can enter an unlimited amount of text – you aren't restricted by space, as you are in a normal, paper diary.

SCHEDULING COMMITMENTS

Diarising appointments

Most people understand the common sense of this. When you have a meeting or appointment, schedule it in the diary. Allow adequate time for travelling there and back at either side, and don't underestimate how long the appointment will take. It is better to overestimate the time, and then if the appointment takes less, you have some unexpected free time to use as you will.

Batching activities

Earlier, we spoke of the advantages of doing small tasks in batches. Diarise time to do these on a regular basis, so they are taken care of. You can even schedule in certain times of the day to make telephone calls: for example, first thing in the morning, and immediately after lunch. Then whenever you get a message to call someone, you simply add it to your list of calls to be made, and deal with it during the next 'telephone time'.

In a similar way, routine correspondence can be dealt with, say, twice a week, depending on how much of it there is.

The basics of scheduling

1. Block out any fixed time commitments, e.g. regular meetings, holidays, organised appointments.

2. Block out some time for living! Eating lunch, coffee, toilet, etc. all take time out of your day, so you need to allow some time for them.

3. Block in some time for planning and scheduling – organising yourself and your day. This needs to be at the beginning or end of each day.

4. Keep flexible. Always allow some time for unexpected events, interruptions, etc. Ideally, two hours a day (or at least one if you really can't) – you can always fill the time with routine work if nothing happens, so don't be alarmed by the thought of blocking out two hours a day.

5. Add in some time for batched tasks, as above – telephone calls, and routine correspondence, plus any other tasks which are part of your job that you can do in batches.

6. Allow time for routine tasks. Perhaps there are some regular updates, reports, or checks which you make weekly, for example. These can be scheduled in for each week on the appropriate time and day.

7. Every day, check your schedule for tomorrow. Is it realistic? Can you achieve it? If not, move things around, reschedule events where you can until it's workable. If you *are* going to have to move things around, don't leave it until the last minute, which can greatly inconvenience others. Do it the day before, so they can reschedule *their* time accordingly as well.

8. Try to plan in variety. For example, don't have a whole day of meetings! This is the idea of batching taken too far, and you will get tired of meeting after meeting, as well as having no time to write up notes or act on what was discussed. Try to batch small tasks, but where you have a lot of similar large tasks, spread them about if you can.

AVOIDING OVERCOMMITMENT

I wish there was an instant cure for overcommitment. Wouldn't it be lovely if whenever you opened your diary or schedule and you saw a week chock-full of things with barely enough time to think about them let alone do them, you could just take two overcommitment tablets and it would all miraculously become manageable. Unfortunately, this isn't possible. The trick to handling over-commitment is to **avoid** it – not to let it happen in the first place.

Avoiding it *is* possible, it just isn't always easy. The following suggestions aren't magic – they won't necessarily work. But if you try to use as many of them as you can, their combined effect should be sufficient to keep your diary and schedule from overflowing on a regular basis.

Being assertive
- Don't be afraid to say 'no'.

- If something isn't your role, but should really be done by someone else, say so.

- If you don't know how to do something, say so.

- If you don't want to do something, say so.

- If you haven't got time, say so.

Controlling your diary/schedule

- Don't be afraid to reschedule things in order to fit in things that are more urgent or important.

- Don't fall into the trap of having too much empty space in a diary or schedule – schedule in the things that *you* know you have to do. There's nothing wrong with scheduling in a lunch break, although very few people do!

- Don't isolate yourself. If you don't leave a diary when you go out, people don't know when you *are* available, and may take the risk of scheduling you for things without checking.

- Don't let others access your diary or schedule unless you can trust them not to book you up for things which you wouldn't do yourself.

Querying people

- Always ask yourself 'Is this really a good use of my time?' If the answer is no, then see whether you really need to do it.

- Always ask other people 'How urgent is this? How important is it?' That way, you can prioritise effectively.

- Ask *when* things need to be done, so you can set deadlines.

- Ask *whether* you need to be at meetings, or to do tasks, if you feel that they aren't a good use of your time.

- Ask *who* else is working on something – maybe you can pool ideas and resources to get a job done in half the time.

- Ask *why* you need to do something if you are not sure whether you should do it or not.

QUESTIONS AND ANSWERS

Surely booking time in my own diary or schedule to do things like make telephone calls is a little bit excessive?

Not at all. You don't have to write 'Do not disturb' in the diary, or 'Telephone calls'. Why not invent some codes, e.g. 'Mr Bell' for telephone calls, or 'Project meeting' when you are working on a major task. That way, no one will think you're being unreasonable, but at the same time you will be in total control of your time.

I try to avoid overcommitment whenever possible. The problem is that sometimes things seem to creep up on me, and I suddenly find myself overwhelmed with meetings, appointments and work – all at once. What can I do about this once it's already happened?

Firstly you need to plan and schedule carefully, so that this doesn't happen often. But given a situation as described here, where it already has, **STOP**. Stop everything, and take time out to plan. When things are so frantic, the natural reaction tends to be to get on and try to clear at least some of the work by getting 'stuck in'. You have to resist this, and take a few moments to think clearly, and plan.

Look at all the meetings and appointments. Is it **essential** that you attend? Can you send someone else? Can you reschedule them? Can you give them a miss altogether? Next, look at the things you are going to avoid as a result – can you get someone else to make the arrangements for you? If so, this will save you more time.

Then look at the workload. Delegate, or get a colleague to cover as much as possible. Can you renegotiate any deadlines (or better still, get anyone else to renegotiate them for you)? Extending deadlines will give you more time **right now**. It is *always* worth checking, even if you don't think this will be possible. Otherwise, you will never know whether the deadline has changed, or the need has become less urgent, or even if the task no longer needs to be done! **Plan before you do anything** – you will probably be surprised by how much difference it can make.

TRAVELLING AND WAITING

Have you ever considered how much time you spend in these two activities? Just think about it:

- arriving early for meetings or appointments
- commuting
- driving
- on the bus, coach or train
- queuing
- time between appointments or meetings
- travelling

- waiting for others who are late

- waiting for transport

and these are only a few of the potential sources of unproductive time!

We all find ourselves in situations like these. So how can we use good time management to benefit from these situations? I'm not advocating that you spend every spare minute of the day working! After all, very few people when asked what they would do differently if they had their lives to live again would say 'spend more time working!'

For some people, these unproductive times are welcome breaks from the hustle and bustle of their working day. Trains are often full of commuters in the mornings and evenings, going to and from work with their head in a book, engrossed in the story. Or they are gazing out of the window daydreaming, or even sleeping. For these people, maybe working on the move isn't a help, but increases their stress levels. Personally, I like to keep work at work, and home at home, and the time spent travelling from one to the other is spent buried in a good book.

But some of us *would* benefit greatly from an extra hour in the day. And for some people, you can find it simply by utilising travelling and waiting time, converting them from unproductive into productive times.

You have two choices:

- to try to avoid waiting time, and

- to plan to use it.

Using waiting and/or travelling time

Being prepared
Try to carry some work around with you, so you can utilise effectively any free time. This doesn't mean carrying armfuls of paper or heavy briefcases. In particular, try to always carry a folder full of reading from your reading pile with you, to read in odd moments. This is one of the best ways to keep on top of your reading. Also, take documents for checking – you can read and check these quickly and easily in a few spare minutes.

Deciding how to travel
Think about **how** you travel, as well as **when**. For example, travelling by

train rather than driving can be more relaxing, less stressful, more predictable and more productive because you can work on the train.

Equipping yourself appropriately

If you have a laptop/portable computer, you can use that to good effect. Consider what other things would help you: a mobile phone, for example.

Getting there early

Optimise waiting time by planning to leave early, and get there early thus taking advantage of the time you will have to yourself before the meeting or appointment starts. A further benefit of this technique is that if you experience delays en route, you will still be on time or just a little late, rather than being seriously delayed.

Knowing what needs doing

You need to be aware of what needs to be done. As a bare minimum, you should aim to carry your To Do list with you everywhere. That way you can use travelling and/or waiting time to make calls, draft correspondence, etc. If nothing else, you can use this usually unproductive time to rewrite your list regularly, a job which often gets overlooked because we can't make the time to do it!

Teaching yourself something new

While travelling, consider listening to business books on cassette, or educational materials. Or read books on management, or other topics relevant to your work.

Avoiding waiting time

Not everyone will want to use their travelling or waiting time, as we have said. Some people would prefer to avoid it, or try to eliminate it as much as possible. So if you go prepared for unexpected delays, and try to eliminate as much waiting and travelling time as possible, you can save time that way.

Confirm appointments and meetings

Confirm appointments before you leave for them. That way, you will eliminate wasted journeys if there has been a mix-up, or if the meeting/appointment has been cancelled or is running late.

Don't be seen to be idle

Do not be seen to get to meetings or appointments too early. When you arrive early, find somewhere else where you can work, use the telephone, or have a coffee and read. If you are seen to be sitting waiting, people often assume you have plenty of time, and they tend to be less concerned about taking up your time, keeping you waiting, etc. in future.

Don't play power games
If people regularly keep you waiting, try to stop them. They may be playing power games with you, or simply being inconsiderate. Here are some suggestions to try to put an end to these games.

● If a meeting or appointment is repeatedly late, ask politely if the other person or people could come to you, so you can avoid being kept waiting.

● If a particular meeting always starts late, get there on time, and then leave a message saying where you can be contacted, and leave the room until you are summoned because everyone is ready to start. This makes the point, politely.

● If you can afford to leave, leave after 15 minutes or so. Say politely that you can't wait, and the meeting or appointment will have to be rescheduled. This conditions people not to keep you waiting in future.

● Work while you are waiting, and when the person you have been waiting for arrives, ask if *they* wouldn't mind waiting for *you*, while you finish what you are doing. Turning the tables on them often prevents them trying to feel more important by keeping you waiting.

CHECKLIST

● Batch activities wherever possible.
● Be assertive in controlling your own diary. Don't be afraid to query people who want some of your time, so you can give their request the right priority.
● Decide whether you will use or avoid waiting time, then act accordingly.
● Don't get carried away – plan before getting caught up in work.

- Don't get caught up in overplanning, so you can't be flexible.
- Don't let people keep you waiting by playing 'power games'.
- Don't waste time travelling or waiting unless you *want* to.
- Keep a diary for scheduling.
- Plan your activities.

CASE STUDIES

Harriet is too busy to plan

Susan was rather pleased that Harriet had found her sorting and list-making so useful, that she continued to use this organised way of operating for quite some time. After about two weeks, though, Harriet was suffering from diary overload again, *and* there were stacks of both urgent and important things piling up. All of a sudden, she reverted to her usual behaviour, and started ploughing through the urgent and important items, in no particular order. Susan tried to persuade her to take some time out to plan, but Harriet found that a waste of time. Things were so disorganised, Harriet missed out on being able to use Susan to get some of the unimportant but urgent tasks out of the way, and in the end, Susan found she was getting in the way, rather than being able to help. So she left Harriet to her own devices.

Larry forgets appointments and deadlines

Larry likes his freedom – he doesn't like using a diary at all. Therefore, he doesn't carry a realistic picture in his head of what he has in terms of available time. A lot of his friends who also work from home on a freelance basis operate similarly – it fits the lifestyle well. He is always forgetting appointments, and if he only realised it, one of the main reasons why he ignores deadlines until the last minute is that he tends to not really have a clear idea about what deadlines he has. If he at least had a list of deadlines to work to, he would be less likely to get into trouble.

Susan keeps Harriet waiting

Susan was supposed to meet Mark and Harriet every Thursday morning, for a regular get-together. Harriet was almost always late, and Susan became fed up of sitting and waiting for her. Sometimes she could get on with her own work, but more often than not, she ended up sitting in Mark's office while he worked, waiting and pouring the coffee. Apart from anything else, it made her feel like a dogsbody, rather than the important member of the team that she was.

The very next time it happened, Susan waited until 9.00am and then stood up. 'Mark, I'm just going back to the office – if you could give me a call when Harriet arrives, I'll come straight back.' Mark smiled. 'Was it my aftershave?' he joked. 'I've just got a few things I can be getting on with,' Susan replied.

When Harriet did arrive, Susan wasn't there, and they had to wait a minute or two while she came down. Although it wasn't long, Harriet was irritated. After a few more times of this treatment, she might arrive on time more often.

DISCUSSION POINTS

1. Examine your diary for the last few months. Where could you have scheduled time for yourself to make life easier?

2. Develop a series of codes for use in your diary so you can book time to work uninterrupted.

5
Delegating

Delegation is giving someone the authority to carry out part of your job for you, or some task that is part of your job.

APPRECIATING THE ADVANTAGES

As we have seen in previous chapters, we want to be **effective**. This means using our time to do the right things. Then, those things we decide we are going to do, we do **efficiently**, which means doing them in the best way. Prioritising and planning have indicated how to deal with those things you *are* going to do. Now you need to know how to handle the things you aren't.

Some of the things you aren't going to do, no one will do: they simply aren't important or urgent, and you need to say 'no' to those things. But others, you are going to get someone else to do for you: you are going to **delegate**.

Delegation is probably the single most important thing you can do to generate more time for yourself. Delegation has several advantages for you and for the other person.

Advantages for you
- You will have more time.

- You will be free – to both concentrate on and do other things.

- You will be protected if you are away: your work can still happen in your absence, with other people carrying on with it.

Advantages for others
- They will develop new skills.

- They will be able to use their existing skills fully.

- They will feel involved, and therefore more satisfied and happy in their work.

- Morale will be good.

- There will be fewer delays while people wait for you to make decisions – they will be able to decide themselves.

DELEGATING PROPERLY

Finding the tasks
How do you decide what to delegate? Earlier chapters may have helped you identify likely tasks. But faced with a list of tasks you should delegate, how do you decide which of the tasks to start with? It's surprisingly simple. Go through the list of tasks that should be delegated, and split them into four categories.

1. Tasks beyond the skills and capabilities of the people – 'tough tasks'
Don't delegate these. Everyone likes a challenge once in a while, but if they get things wrong, and/or fail at the task, it will only demotivate them, and may make them wary of being delegated to again.

2. Tasks so crucial that failure would cause huge problems – 'critical tasks'
It's not fair to give these tasks to people, unless you are absolutely sure they can do the job, to the required standard, and by the deadline. Otherwise, these are tasks you need to keep yourself.

3. Tasks that have been delegated to you
If someone has delegated something to you, it is probably because they feel *you* are the right person for the task. It is best to check before delegating these tasks on to others. There may be some good reason that you are not aware of as to why *you* in particular have to do this particular task.

4. Everything else
These are the tasks you will delegate. You will usually find that these tasks fall into several categories themselves:

- routine tasks, carried out at regular intervals

- tasks requiring no special skills – easy tasks

- time-consuming tasks

- tasks planned for some time in the future, but that are not pressing just yet

• tasks requiring specialist knowledge or skill.

There are others, but this gives you a few examples of the sorts of things that might be available for you to delegate.

Finding the people

Now you need to decide **who** to delegate to. The only person to avoid is someone who is so busy with their own work that they are unable to take on anything else. Everyone else can be delegated to (provided you have the authority to do so).

Routine tasks can be delegated to someone with a steady workload, so they can plan in the additional work. Tasks requiring no special skills can be delegated to someone junior, to give them a little more responsibility, and to make them feel more valued. Time-consuming tasks can be given to people with the capacity to take on more work, or those who like work involving attention to detail. Also, you could give these tasks to people who can delegate themselves, so they can delegate some of their own work while they do the time-consuming task itself. Tasks requiring specialist skills or knowledge can obviously go to those people who have that knowledge or skill — or you could train someone else, so that more people have the necessary skills and knowledge.

Select a person for a particular task based on the following questions:

• Do they have the time to do the task?

• Do they have the ability?

• If not, can you train/coach them?

• Would they enjoy it?

Do not ignore the last question. No one likes to work with or for someone that gives them all the rotten jobs – and the definition of a rotten job is one you don't like doing. You can't overestimate the effect on morale if you give people work they like doing on a regular basis. And if you don't know what they like doing, ask them!

Now you have identified the task and the person, you are ready to start delegating.

Communicating

Communicating the task
Tell them what the task is, and why you are delegating it. Encourage them to take ownership of the job.

Communicating the limits
You cannot give someone **responsibility**. That is a myth. What you can give someone is **accountability** – the ability to be held accountable for the job, the authority to do the job. Responsibility is something you keep when delegating – because after all, the task is part of *your* job. You are responsible for the task being done correctly. You can make the other person accountable to you, but it is still your responsibility to ensure everything happens the way it is supposed to. Some people will take responsibility for the job, but that doesn't mean you can give up your own responsibility for it. No, that would be abdication, not delegation!

You need to agree what support, help, advice, etc. you will provide to the person you are delegating to. Do they need any training? Resources? Additional help? It is no good someone coming to you and explaining that they cannot complete the task if you have then filled your time with other tasks, so you cannot take it back or help. So agree what help, etc. they need to do the job beforehand, so you can plan accordingly.

Tell others that you are delegating the task, and who to. That way, people know that the person doing the task has your backing, and the authority to get what they need.

Communicating standards, progress and deadlines
You need to be absolutely clear as to what the task being delegated means, and communicate this to the other person.

- What standard is it to be carried out to?

- What progress checks will you be making?

- What is the deadline?

You can do this by setting objectives. An objective is an agreed specification for a piece of work. For example:

> *to calculate by next Friday the budget spent so far this year under all categories, by cost centre, and to summarise this on one sheet, in as much detail as the size will allow.*

As you can see, this is a quite detailed matter – far more complicated than just saying 'John, can you get me a budget analysis by next Friday?' Proper objectives are SMART:

S – Specific
M – Measurable
A – Achievable
R – Realistic
T – Time-related (i.e. with a deadline)

Writing down the task as an objective is rather like a contract between you and the other person – a contract for the work. You wouldn't dream of saying to a builder 'Put me up a fence, will you?' and letting him get on with it. No way! You'd want to know how high, what fencing, when it would be finished, how much it would cost – all sorts of things. Treat people in the same way when you delegate to them. Give them all the information they need to give you exactly what you want from them, but without being so incredibly specific they can't exercise their own judgment, initiative or creativity. Try to leave them enough leeway to decide for themselves **how** they are going to achieve the objective.

Letting them get on with it
So, having briefed people properly, you don't just sit back and let them get on with it: now you have to make sure they carry on with the task without problems.

Giving support
Some people will go off and do things happily, others will feel they need support and advice. Whilst you should aim to give these when necessary, beware of people who never seem to be able to manage without them. Some people have a lack of confidence which prompts them to keep checking that they are doing things correctly. They may need extra encouragement, to try to stop this habit. Alternatively, try referring them to someone else, so they don't get dependent on you. And don't forget to offer support even to those who don't seem to need it – some people are afraid to ask for help.

Monitoring progress
Monitoring is not checking. Monitoring means watching – seeing what is being done, and asking people how they are getting on. It does not mean examining their part-finished work regularly to look

for mistakes. If you are monitoring properly, you won't get too many mistakes – you will spot things and be able to intervene gently before they arise. Try to be available, not to lurk watchfully as if you are expecting things to go wrong. Just knowing that someone is there if they need them gives people confidence.

Stepping in

If you do have to step in because you can see that things are starting to go wrong, tread carefully. The last thing you should do is to take back the job – even though they may want you to! Talk things over and leave them to get on with it again, this time aware of where they were starting to go wrong. Delegation is highly dependent on confidence to succeed – so never undermine people's confidence by threatening to take back the work, or worse, to get someone else to take it over. Even if they think they can't carry on with it, try to support them and let them try again. This lets them know you trust them to do good work.

Evaluating success

Once the delegated task is finished, try to have a review with the person who did it, even if it is only a few minutes. Check whether the objective has been met, and if not, why not. Find out how the other person found the task. They may need further training, or you may learn more about how to delegate in future.

Of course, you could just look at the task and see whether it has been done well – without involving the other person. But feedback helps them to improve, and to know whether they have done well.

QUESTIONS AND ANSWERS

I ask people to do things all the time. Isn't that delegating?

No. Delegating is giving someone part of your own job to do, not just any task that needs to be done – it has to be part of your job. A receptionist asking someone to get her a file isn't delegating. But asking someone to take over the reception desk while she goes and looks for the file is – because covering the desk is her job.

Won't all this take so long I would have been quicker doing it myself?

Perhaps at first. But once you get used to delegating, you will do it more quickly, and once others get used to you delegating tasks to them, they will get better at them, so things will speed up.

Remember, in the long term, you will have far more free time as the delegatable parts of your job are done by others.

Isn't that a bit of a cheek, asking other people to do part of my job?

No – you are simply making time for all the things you can do better than them. Imagine a world where everyone did what they could do best, and no one had to waste time doing things they did badly, or that took them ages to achieve. Well, you can move some way towards that. And always remember, most people *want* to progress – if they learn part of your job, they are learning new tasks, and progressing.

WATCHING OUT FOR PROBLEMS

So, if delegation is so wonderful, why don't people do it all the time? Obviously, there are also some disadvantages. These can easily be avoided, if you are aware of them and plan accordingly when you delegate.

Disadvantages of delegating

- You may be afraid of losing control. You can avoid this by making the limits of authority of everyone involved clear, and monitoring them regularly. Be careful not to overcheck – this can make people feel you don't trust them.

- You may be afraid that the quality of the work will suffer. One of the most common barriers to delegation is the worry that other people can't do something as well as you can. They never will, unless you let them try and practise! Investing time now in showing them how to do a task properly will save you much more time in the longer term.

- Sometimes, people may keep checking back to ask how they are doing, how they should proceed, etc. This can be avoided by briefing them properly, and making sure they know you are there if they need you. Encourage 'management by exception', where people only come to you if things aren't going well or according to plan; otherwise they just keep up the good work.

- Some people may feel resentful – burdened by the extra work in addition to their own. Make sure delegation is always fair: it may be tempting to give work to the same people all the time because you know they will do it well, but others need to learn how to do tasks as well. Make sure you don't overload people.

- You may secretly be afraid the other person may do the task as well as you. Well, let them! If they do the things *they* can do well, this frees your time to concentrate on the things which *you* do well. This is good for morale, and gives everyone a chance to perform at their best – efficiency.

- You may feel you don't have time to delegate. Well, if you don't make time, you never will. Nothing about your workload will change unless you make some changes. You are **investing** time when you delegate: you will get it back in the long term.

- There may be parts of your job you don't want to delegate, even though you could. Perhaps these are the parts you enjoy doing. Well, no one says you have to delegate all of them. Keep some of the things you enjoy for yourself, and delegate others. That way, you can enjoy yourself without having the added stress of accumulating work and time pressure.

CHECKLIST

- Only do the things you **should** be spending your time on – delegate the rest.

- Don't delegate difficult or crucial tasks unless you are sure they are within people's capabilities.

- As far as possible, try to delegate tasks so people do things they enjoy, that motivate them, or that develop their skills.

- Give people both the authority to do the task, and the support they need to get it done.

- Set SMART objectives.

- Don't be so prescriptive that you stifle people's own judgment, initiative or credibility.

- If you have to step in, do it carefully, so others don't lose confidence.

- Give feedback to people after the task is complete.

- Overcome any fears you have of losing control, of competition, of failure to get the job done, etc.

CASE STUDIES

Harriet abdicates rather than delegates

Harriet came out of a late meeting that had over-run, to find everyone else had gone home. She took the time to check her messages and in-tray, and found a couple of really urgent matters that needed doing the next day without fail. She scribbled a note on a piece of paper, paperclipped it to the papers, and left it all on Susan's desk. Susan would sort it out, she knew she could rely on her.

In the morning, Harriet was at a briefing session, and popped out during the coffee break to call Susan to check. The line was engaged, and she forgot to keep trying when she caught sight of someone she needed to speak with about something else.

Susan was on a training course all day, so those really urgent matters didn't get dealt with, and Harriet arrived back at the office at around 3.00pm to find the papers still on Susan's desk. If only she had checked that Susan would be able to do the tasks before she delegated them (not that you can call Harriet's note delegating).

Larry is late with a deadline

Larry had asked his publishers to do some diagrams for the latest book he was working on, as he was handling several projects at once. Richard at the publishers agreed to help with this, as although Larry had always done his own in the past, they were able to produce them just as easily. So Larry sent Richard a specific list of what he wanted, and then checked all was well in a phone call. 'You know the sort of thing I'm looking for, Richard – the diagrams I usually do; nothing fancy. No rush – the deadline's a while yet.'

After a while, he had finished the manuscript and sent it off, with a note that Richard would have the diagrams for insertion. But Richard hadn't done them quite as Larry had envisaged, and there was a delay while they were sorted out. Larry vowed never to trust anyone else with anything important again. If he had monitored Richard, and checked whether he was doing all right from time to time, there wouldn't have been the mix-up.

Susan struggles with overload

Susan returned after her training course to find a whole lot of routine, time-consuming work from Harriet (obviously left so Harriet could catch up on more important things). There was far too much to do when added to her own work, so Susan went to another section which had a student on a work placement. She negotiated some of the student's time, and together they went through the tasks and decided which ones Mike, the student, could handle. Mike went back to his section with a pile of papers, and Susan and he met daily to check progress.

 Mike was happy because any problems or queries that he had were answered at the next meeting, and Susan knew she could leave Mike to get on with things because he couldn't progress too far in the wrong direction between meetings. Mike gained some new skills and experience which stood him in good stead when he went back to college.

DISCUSSION POINTS

1. Try to assess in advance what tasks people might be interested in taking on.

2. Make a list of what tasks people are already doing that have been delegated in the past – often once the delegation works, both parties forget it was previously your work.

3. Think about a problem you have had with a delegated task in the past – either delegating to someone else, or being delegated to. How could this have been overcome?

6
Dealing with Physical Organisation

THE PAPER MOUNTAIN

For most people, one of the most daunting things about getting organised is the mountain of paperwork they currently have waiting for them. This paper mountain can often be a molehill in disguise, when you actually go through it and analyse what the paper consists of and exactly what you need to do with it. Just getting the paper rationalised into some sort of system can bring intense relief from the worry of having all that accumulated paperwork to deal with, and no logical start point.

Coping with multiple piles
Sorting papers and items on your desk and surroundings into piles for dealing with later is common practice. A common piece of advice used in time management to counteract this is to handle each piece of paper only once, or **do it now**. For example, if you receive a letter which needs a reply, as soon as you pick up the letter and read it, write the reply. It saves time and keeps the recipient of your extremely speedy response happy. But what about all the other, more important things lower down in your in-tray: things that may have been far more urgent or important than that letter?

Using the two-pile system
It may be preferable for you to handle each piece of paper twice: once to sort it based on its priority, and then once to deal with it when its turn comes round. I tend to adopt this approach: I sort everything into just two piles.

The first contains things that have to be done before I go home, leave work, or sleep (depending *where* I'm working!). They are **immediate** tasks. The second pile is everything else. You could call them TODAY and LATER. But of course, I cheat: if I can quickly deal with something and pass it on, file it, put it in my reading drawer, etc., I do. Some things get processed quickly and painlessly, and never end up in either pile. This way, both piles aren't unmanageable.

When you've finished pile 1, simply tackle as much as you can of pile 2. Then, the next day, you need to re-sort: some of the things in pile 2 that weren't urgent yesterday may need to be transferred into pile 1. It's a good way of ensuring you don't miss deadlines.

The other advantage of this practice is that it helps others. If someone has something that they need you to do urgently, they can place it in pile 1 if you're away from your desk. A good example would be signing letters. A bundle of letters to be signed would generally either be dealt with first to get them out of the way, or consigned to pile 2. But if someone needs them signing so they can go out that day, they can put them in pile 1, and you will know they're more urgent, and make sure you do them that day.

Dealing with the backlog

Most people have a backlog – few people have the luxury of getting all their work done every day, so nothing is ever carried forward. But don't be tempted to leave anything so long that it takes longer to deal with in the long run. Leaving things longer can often involve additional work when you *do* get around to them, and this means using more of your time.

Also, every time you sift through your work and sort it, you're adding to the time it takes next time around, if you keep a lot of items to be sifted. Periodically, clear out backlogs, and deal with long-standing tasks rather than anything else. This will ease your mind as well as reducing the backlog. The real harm in backlogs is that they mentally and emotionally weigh you down, not that they take up too much space in your in-tray.

CLEARING DESKS

Why is it that some people always seem to have neat, tidy desks, whilst others have a shambles of paper piled high, and dotted with various bits and bobs? Well, it isn't because the fairies come in every night and mess up your desk, is it? Some of us just don't seem to be able to keep a clear desk.

A cluttered, untidy desk usually doesn't indicate an excess of work to be done: it indicates poor organisation. Too often, people use the amount of work which they have (especially paperwork) to excuse cluttered desks. But the more work you have, the more important it is to get your desk **organised**.

Given that having a tidy and/or clear desk is something that many of us find difficult, how can we improve? And why *should* we? Firstly, let's establish something very important that it's all too easy to forget. **Your desk is for working on.** Your desk is not:

- a coffee table

- a filing area

- a storage area

- something to sit on.

Disadvantages of an untidy and/or cluttered desk

- Cluttered desks can lead to more error.

- Cluttered desks slow down progress and work.

- Distraction is increased.

- It is harder to establish priorities.

- People judge with their eyes. Untidy desks tend to make people assume you have an untidy mind, poor self-discipline, etc.

- Procrastination is easier if you have a lot of things to deal with before you can get started. Untidiness actually *helps* procrastination, by giving you lots of potential things to do to avoid doing the task in hand.

- You can't find what you want when you want it.

Clearing your desk

Clearing a desk is easy. **Keeping** it clear is the hard part! Here are some rules which should help.

- Handle work as **few times** as possible.

- Have **one tray** (and one tray only) for incoming work. Do not let anyone put things on your desk: make it clear that incoming things belong in the tray. This means that you don't lose control over where things are.

- **Never store things** on your desk. Get them off the desk and to a place where you can get to them again when you need to.

- **Sort incoming work**, and store things not requiring your immediate attention away from your desk.

- **Throw things away**! All too often we hold onto paperwork just in case we ever need it. Be ruthless! Only keep what you *really* need.

- Try to allocate a **small amount of time** at regular intervals, say once a month, to clear your desk and get things back on an even keel. Despite all our best intentions, work builds up, and so does clutter: so programme in a tidy-up at regular intervals.

- Understand that volume of work is not the biggest problem: it's **organisation**.

ORGANISING SHELVES AND STORAGE

Now you have organised most aspects of your immediate work space. Given that we said above your desk is not a storage space, you do need to give some thought to your shelves and storage areas.

Break the work down

We have advocated breaking tasks and goals down. Do the same with organising your physical space. Do one part of the job at a time, and programme it around other work. That way, you won't get behind in your work while you spring-clean, neither will the organising be put off because it is too large and daunting a task.

Break the area down

Break your work area down into areas – just as you break big tasks down into small ones, to make them easier to handle. Your desk is one easy area to see – now identify other areas:

- bookshelves
- computer workstation
- cupboards
- desk
- drawers
- filing cabinet(s)
- shelves
- tables
- tops of filing cabinets.

Making life easy – keeping things to hand

Decide which things you need to use or refer to most often. It makes sense to have these things closest to hand, to make your life as easy as possible. I know one colleague who keeps their stapler, hole punch and ruler in a cupboard on the other side of the room! Every time they need to use one of these items, they get up from their desk, cross the room, open the cupboard, get the item out, use it, replace it, close the cupboard and get back to work. I wonder how many times a day they repeat this?

Grouping items

It's amazing how often the same principles come up time and again in time management. Just as we said batch tasks for efficiency, batch or group items together for ease of usage. Try to establish broad categories of things that can be grouped together. For example, here are some categories – but remember, this is not an exhaustive list – you will have your own things:

- catalogues
- company information
- computer books/manuals
- files
- magazines and professional papers
- notes
- reading materials
- reference manuals
- reports
- stationery
- telephone directories.

Be ruthless!

- Anything you haven't used for two or three weeks can safely be stored.
- Banish personal photographs, knick-knacks, etc. They don't have to disappear: transfer them to a shelf or cupboard – not on your desk itself, which is for **work**.
- Don't be afraid to put things away.

- Duplicates can be safely thrown away.

- Little items such as stapler, hole punch, staple remover, Tippex, etc. can be placed in a drawer – not out on your desk where they can get in the way and make you feel cluttered.

- Outdated information should be obtained in a more up-to-date form, or discarded altogether.

- Put all personal items – coffee stocks, toiletries, spare socks, umbrella, etc. to one place, preferably a drawer.

- Spend a few minutes at the end of every week (preferably every day) to tidy your workspace. By keeping on top of things in this way, they don't build up and take ages to sort out again.

- Things that have not been referred to for a month or more can be stored away – in a cupboard or filing system. They don't need to be (and shouldn't be) in sight.

Finally, ask yourself 'what's the worst thing that could happen if I threw this away?' If you can live with the answer, then throw it!

QUESTIONS AND ANSWERS

I have to confess, I get a little nervous about throwing things away. Do I have to?

Of course not. How about this technique: if you aren't sure, store it all in a box – a photocopying or paper box is ideal. Once a month, go through the box and see how you feel. Anything that you now feel needs filing, file. Anything you now feel you won't need again, throw away. Anything you're still unsure of goes back in the box! Feel better now?

I like my desk like this – I know where everything is!

I wish I had a pound for every time I have heard this. 'I like a fairly cluttered desk – it's not efficient, but I just *like* it that way!' But do you want to save yourself time or not? Let me ask you another important question: do you *really* know where everything is? Can you *really* find it all quickly and easily? Most people who think they can are surprised when this is put to the test. They don't realise just how disorganised they have become. Unless you try being tidy and organised, you won't know whether it will improve things or not. So why not give it a try?

HANDLING CLUTTER

Clutter isn't just paper. It's all sorts of things: a coat over the back of a chair rather than hung up; papers spilling out of a waste bin; old coffee cups; dead flowers or plants in vases or pots; packaging from parcels or correspondence that has been opened; magazines; useful papers that you think you should hang on to in case they come in handy – the list is endless.

Clutter is disorder. But it's more than just a mess – the word clutter means a mess or disorder that interferes with other things. In technical terminology, clutter is the word used to mean the shadows on radar pictures caused by old radar signals (or 'blips') that interfere in the picture. Clutter gets in the way. Handling clutter isn't about being tidy, it's about being free to do work without interference from things in the way.

Spotting clutter

Paper
This is what most people think of when they think of clutter: piles of paper.

- Don't keep what you don't need.

- File things whenever you can, to get them out of the way.

- File things where you can find them when you need them.

- Look realistically at things already filed and stored, and assess regularly whether you still need them.

Electronic clutter
I don't mean radar screen clutter, I mean saved files and e-mails. The electronic office is great for some, but for others, it just replaces the misery of an overflowing in-tray and desk with an overflowing mailbox and computer screen.

- Be ruthless.

- File what you need to keep so it's out of sight but retrievable.

- Label things sensibly and meaningfully so they are easy to find.

- Don't send to more people than necessary when you send out your own e-mails – it only passes the clutter on!

● Don't be afraid to delete – it's quite painless (most of the time!)

Other stuff
This includes the coffee cups, the coats, the spare tissues, the odds and ends. All the things you would tidy away if you were having important visitors, in fact. Why not expect an important visitor every day – you! Important because you will do a full day's work, unrestricted and uncluttered by all those things. It's certainly a thought.

Reducing clutter

Loose papers
File them. If there isn't a file, create one. Filing will be discussed in the next chapter.

Items waiting
By this, I mean waiting for other people to make decisions before these things can be actioned. Keep these to hand if the answer is expected imminently – today or tomorrow, say. If the response is likely to take longer, consider a file called 'awaiting response'. Then when you get the response, you can take the appropriate action, and transfer the paperwork into the correct subject file.

Little pieces of paper – notes or sticky post-its
Throw them away if they've been dealt with. Don't be tempted to keep notes on scraps of paper just because they have useful details or contact numbers on – these should be transferred to somewhere safer. Things on scraps of paper aren't safe, they are too easily lost. Consider establishing a 'To Do' system instead, and do away with all the notes.

Interesting things you don't know what to do with
File them. If you don't know how, set up a file called something like 'interesting bits and pieces', and keep them all in there!

Papers pending your decision
These should be in one of your trays – to get actioned.

Forms
Keep all these together in one place – consider a file just for forms.

CHECKLIST

* At the end of each day, take just a couple of minutes to clear things away – have a tidy-up. This tends to stop things accumulating.

CASE STUDIES

Harriet

Harriet's problem is her paper mountain. It's so huge that she virtually never tackles it. Very occasionally, she comes in on a Sunday, when it's quiet, and has a blitz on everything. This usually results in Susan coming in to an overflowing in-tray on the Monday morning!

The problem is that by the time Harriet finds half of her paper, it's too late to action it, or if she needs some information, she often has to find it again, as she has lost what she was originally sent. If she only sorted more regularly, she would manage her workload far more easily. Few people take 'time out' to see what actually needs doing at regular intervals – it's far more tempting to 'get stuck in' – like Harriet – which isn't always effective.

Larry

Larry's problem is the opposite. He has everything tidy and put away. He has so few reminders of work around him that it's easy to forget things. Each working session starts with 'getting ready', and finding the things he needs before he can actually start work. And then afterwards, he always stop ten minutes or so before he needs to, to 'tidy up' and put everything away. This probably sounds completely out of character for a person as laid-back as Larry. He says it is necessary as he works from home, but really he could leave work laid out in his office – a converted spare room – it certainly wouldn't be in the way. He is actually using the rituals of organisation as a neat way to procrastinate. It's really all about spending time organising so that he has less time to spend actually working.

Susan

Susan, as one would expect, is organised. She has systems for putting things away so they are easily retrievable – but unfortunately, Harriet doesn't understand them and so gets easily frustrated. Also, Susan is rather scared of losing things, and so she tends to retain huge quantities of paper copies of things – just so Harriet can find copies when she loses her own. What would be *really* organised would be for her to sit down with Harriet and agree the organisation of the office. Then Harriet would know where everything is, and wouldn't spend so much time rummaging for things.

It's too easy to be organised yourself, but leaving everyone else unable to find a thing! You need to make your systems public, so others know where things are, and they will then be encouraged to co-operate.

DISCUSSION POINTS

1. Make a series of appointments with yourself on a regular basis to get organised. You don't have to have a long session and get everything done in one go – make an action plan of tackling different areas of your physical workplace, and getting them all sorted appropriately.

2. Take an inventory of people's desks that you see. How do they look? Do they seem effective? Can you learn from anyone?

3. Establish a half-way house for your rubbish bin. Set up a box or shelf and use this for a month to store all the papers, leaflets, information, etc. that you aren't sure you need to keep but are worried about discarding. At the end of the month, go through the items, and discard what you now feel comfortable with. Do this every two weeks or so from now on. You will find that you become more ruthless about throwing things away that aren't needed.

7
Dealing with Paperwork and Admin

FILING

Filing is something so simple that most of us do it without much
thought. But often, people have poor practices to do with filing, and
these can cost us valuable time. Do you do any of these?

- Filing things by date rather than by subject.
- Having lots of small files (too many).
- Having only a few huge files (too few).
- Keeping files indefinitely.
- Never discarding or archiving old filing.
- Not keeping filing up-to-date.
- Not labelling files with a meaningful name or reference.
- Not remembering where you filed something.

Methods of filing
There are several methods of filing, and you need to use the most
appropriate one for the material you want to file:

- by subject
- by alphabetical reference, usually names or places
- by number
- by area
- by date.

General filing principles
- All files should be named. Give files or folders a name that is

meaningful, so when you see the name, you logically think of things that would go in that particular file.

- Always use a wide subject for a file name. By a wide subject, I mean a subject that doesn't just contain a few areas: thick files are easier to deal with by looking through them for something, than lots of thin files, which you have to search between as you aren't sure which one the document may be in. Use wide categories, or large subjects, wherever possible.

- Colour code files and labels where possible, to make it easy to see at a glance which file you need.

- Don't file things that you can easily get from someone else when needed. This is one of the most common bad filing habits, and only leads to enlarging your filing system unnecessarily.

- File odds and ends according to the information they contain, not where you found them. This includes magazine articles, interesting snippets, etc. For example, file articles and papers about management under 'management', rather than by the magazine or training course they came from.

- File things within folders or files with the most recent thing on top. This will make it easier to find. Filing like this, in date order, should be used wherever possible.

- Set up a regular time to go through files and get rid of old and unwanted material, so they don't just keep growing bigger and bigger.

- Store files within your filing system alphabetically, as a general rule. If there are one or two files which you use very frequently, maybe you would be better to keep these in an easily accessible place. Similarly, if a few files are used regularly by others, it might be wise to put these somewhere prominent, where they can be easily found without rummaging through your other files. But otherwise, order your files in alphabetical order.

- Use file names that are nouns, also called naming words. Do not use file names that are verbs, or doing words. For example:

'contracts' not 'negotiating'

'vacancies' not 'recruiting'.

- Use the first association your mind makes when you think of the things in the file. This means that when you are looking for something, your thought process should usually be the same, and you will be most likely to deduce in which file the document will be.

- When unsure whether you need to file something or not, put it in a drawer, box or tray for a month. If you haven't needed to refer to it in that time, it's usually safe to think about filing it.

DEALING WITH MAIL IN AND OUT

Mail coming in can't be controlled: you can't keep it away from you when you're busy. So, you need efficient systems for handling mail, so it doesn't take up more of your time than it deserves. Every day, sort through incoming mail and/or paperwork. This will mean looking through your in-tray at least once a day.

Don't be tempted to think that other things are more important than 'going through the post' – this is one of the most common management mistakes. After all, how do you know that something more important and urgent than your most important and/or urgent work hasn't just arrived? Or you could be wasting time doing something important, while instructions to do it differently (or not to do it at all) are sitting in your in-tray.

Problems with in-trays

- An in-tray used for you to put things in as a reminder - so it is used as a notice board or To Do list.

- An in-tray which becomes a filing system.

- An in-tray which never seems to get any smaller.

- An overflowing in-tray.

- Not having one.

- Only going through it once a week.

- Sorting your in-tray and putting things back in it at the bottom.

- The whole of your desk being an in-tray.

Sorting mail in

There are two main ways to sort mail. Firstly, sort it by priority. Use the important v. urgent guidelines to establish which things are the highest priority. Then within each priority, sort things so like tasks are together.

Prioritising on the basis of importance and urgency isn't foolproof – nothing is. But for most people, it's a good system to rely on. Sorting incoming mail and tasks so like things are together means that you can 'batch' things – you can do things in batches. Working by doing things in batches is efficient. It tends to make work faster and easier. For example, group all letters to be written together, and all phone calls to be made together, etc. Then you can concentrate on one job at a time, and spend a period of time making calls, a period of time writing letters, reading, signing things, etc.

Remember the two-pile system

When you go through your tray, everything you pick up must either (1) be dealt with then and there, (2) go into the 'today' pile, or (3) go into the 'later' pile. Here are some examples:

Deal with immediately
This doesn't mean filing documents or reading them immediately – it simply means dealing with them immediately by getting them out of the in-tray and preferably off your desk.

- Filing goes straight into a filing storeplace for (at least) weekly filing.

- Items for future dates go straight into the 'day file' (see later).

- Items for passing on go straight out.

- Items for reading go straight into your reading storeplace.

- Unwanted items are discarded.

Today pile

- Correspondence that must be replied to today.

- Messages to be replied to today.

- Papers that must be read or gone through before today's meetings.

- Papers that come out of the day file today (see later).

Note: the word **today** appears in every item. If it can wait, it goes in the Later pile.

Later pile
- Correspondence that you need to think about.

- Non-urgent work.

- Papers to go into the day file for other days (see later).

- Things you aren't sure what to do with.

- What's left after you have removed the 'do now' and 'today' things.

Understanding the advantages
Sorting tasks and mail in gives you one huge advantage. It lets you plan your day. When you have sorted, you know what the day holds in store for you (apart from the unforeseen emergencies and interruptions). Even the unforeseen interruptions and emergencies can be planned for, by leaving a little time unscheduled to make enough free time available to deal with them if they occur. And if they don't happen, you can just use the time to do more routine work.

Being ruthless
Never forget, the whole point of going through the mail in is to **reduce** it. Anything that can be passed on, put to one side for filing, filed, discarded or sent back should be done straight away. By hanging on to these things and dealing with them later, you are delaying the action they need, and also, you end up handling these items more than once. If you have the time, just handle them once and get rid of them.

USING DAY FILES

It is useful to operate with a day file system. This is sometimes called a 'tickler' file by Americans. It's a file specially to remind you of future events, and to hold the papers for these events.

Often in our work, we receive things that we know we will need in the future, but don't need yet. These need to be stored in a safe place, where we can find them when we need them quickly and easily. The obvious place is to have one file set aside solely for such items.

Creating a day file

Have a ring-bound folder which has two sets of file dividers in it. One set is numbered 1 to 31, and another is a set of twelve, labelled for each month of the year. These types of file dividers can be easily purchased in most good stationers.

Suppose the date is 1 January. You should put the 31 numbered file dividers at the front, followed by the twelve month dividers, starting with February and finishing with January. A typical layout is shown in Figure 5.

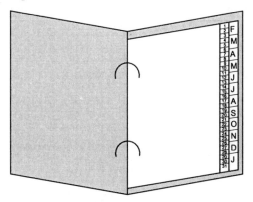

Fig. 5. Typical day file.

Every time you need to put a piece of paper away for a future date, simply file it in the appropriate date: 1–31 if it is required for January, and under the appropriate month if it is required *after* January. Every day, you just check to see what things are there for you.

At the end of the month, you simply remove all February's papers and file them by day appropriately, and place the February divider to the back of the file. This cycles the paperwork on a regular basis, so it doesn't get lost.

Examples of things that you would file in a day file are:

- agendas for meetings
- documents you have been asked to take to an appointment
- letters that have to be replied to by a certain date
- letters that need to be sent on a certain date
- lists of things to be done on that date
- maps and directions for getting to an appointment

- notes you have made for a meeting or appointment

- social invitations.

QUESTIONS AND ANSWERS

I get lots of papers for meetings – agendas for them, and papers to be read or referred to. These don't always come at the same time – they arrive in dribs and drabs. How can I manage these efficiently?

This is exactly the sort of thing that day files were invented for – set up a day file and you should have no problems managing your papers.

What are you saying I actually need? You seem to refer to reading, filing, in-trays – all sorts of things?

What you actually need is one tray – your in-tray. You then remove things from this and put them in two piles – for 'today' and 'later'. You can have another two trays for these piles if you like, as long as people don't get confused and put things which should go into the in-tray into one of the others. You then need some places where you keep filing to be filed, and reading to be read. Again, you can have trays for this, but boxes, drawers, folders etc. are all adequate – or even just a little shelf space!

MANAGING YOUR READING

Don't read things when you get them. Unless something is high enough priority that you need to read it straight away in order to take action, leave it for reading. Then in an ideal world, you can allocate a little time each day for reading. For most of us, this is a luxury we would be hard pressed to achieve! But try to set aside a 'reading time' every week (or twice a week if you have a lot of reading to do at work) of, say, half an hour – longer if you can manage it. This will ensure reading doesn't accumulate to the point that you lose the ability to catch up.

Sorting your reading
Take time to **sort** your reading – never just dig into the reading pile and start from the top down. Sorting your reading needs some thought. Use four categories, and sort before you do anything else.

Items to be retained but not actually read
You don't actually have to read your reading? That sounds a little like
cheating, doesn't it? But there is an enormous quantity of stuff that
you may need to keep for reference, but until you need it there's no
point in reading it. You may even have forgotten the information
before you need it if you read it now. These items should be filed,
unread, by subject – so you can refer to them when you need the
information.

Reading to be read
Some of the reading material you *will* want to read. Put this to one
side, ready. You can take some of this with you when you go to
meetings, or are travelling, to use any spare time profitably. Don't
actually start reading until you've finished sorting. When you do
actually read it, afterwards you need to decide whether to keep it in
a file, or just to discard it.

Material to be passed on
Often, material is of more use to someone else than to you. So pass
it on.

Material for discarding
Some material may turn out to be not worth reading after all, or out
of date by the time you get round to sorting your reading. It can be
discarded. The more you discard, the less the reading pile grows, so
the easier it is to sort: it's all related.

Prune your reading
Don't actually keep the whole thing unless it's necessary. If you
need to read an article in a magazine, or a part of a paper, just keep
the part you need. That way, you won't feel intimidated by the size
of your reading pile. The best thing to do is to make sure you've
skimmed through the *whole* magazine or paper (so you don't miss
anything), then extract the article(s) you want to read, and consign
the rest to the waste paper basket.

   Generally speaking, cutting articles out is quicker than photocopying them, but if you may want to file them, photocopies can be
neater.

Mark up your reading as you read
When you do start to read, read **actively**. All too often, we think of
reading as a passive process, where we sit and let the words enter our

eyes and trickle through to the brain! You can help yourself read by helping the brain to latch on to important facts, words and phrases. Making reading an active process means the brain doesn't switch off so easily, so you are less likely to suffer lack of concentration.

To help you read actively, you can:

- annotate
- highlight
- make notes
- underline.

Consider photocopying a document if you need to, so you can do the above, if the document isn't yours to write on. Especially useful is photocopying things at a slightly reduced size. This gives you a larger margin for making notes, etc. (although beware of making them too hard to read).

Read in as much depth as you need

This means reading the amount of detail *you* need, not the amount that the writer happens to have given in the text. If you only need a feel of the subject, skim through quickly, noting anything that 'jumps out at you'. If you need to read a document properly, wait until you can give it your full attention. And then it's best to skim through first, before reading it 'properly', to get a general feel for what's in the document.

Reading newspapers and magazines

Advantages of articles

Magazines and newspapers have one big advantage: they break a subject down into bite-sized amounts to be read. Reading one article on a subject takes far less time than reading a whole report or book. Also, they tend to look attractive – especially magazine articles, which often include pictures, charts and diagrams to stimulate your interest.

Disadvantages of articles

One of the disadvantages of articles is that they may not give you all the information you want. Also, they often take a useful topic, and pad it out with a lot of other text that you don't need – typically to make it look more attractive and interesting.

CHECKLIST

- Always file in date order whenever possible.

- Keep on top of your mail in and in-tray.

- Keep filing up-to-date – this will save you time in the long run.

- Name and code files where possible (e.g. colour coding).

- Read actively.

- Sort work before you get started.

- Sort your reading, so you have some to take with you when leaving the office for appointments, etc. Prune before reading.

- Use day files if you have time- or date-related papers to handle.

- Use the most appropriate filing method for the material to be filed.

- Watch your filing – don't let it become unmanageable.

CASE STUDIES

Harriet can't find her papers
Harriet is always looking for the things she needs to take to meetings. She has such an overloaded desk, and an in-tray that rarely gets fully examined, so this is hardly surprising. She spends a lot of her time just looking for papers to work on and take with her to appointments. A day file would greatly help her here, but she seems too disorganised to keep one well-maintained. Susan did set one up for her once, but Harriet came in one day while Susan was at lunch, couldn't find her papers for a meeting, was very late by the time she *did* find them in the day file, so triumphantly emptied the entire day file contents back into her in-tray so this couldn't happen again. If only she could be just a little more organised, she would be able to cope.

Larry needs to sort and mark his reading
Larry has an awful lot of material to be read as research for his books. He often has books by other people, magazine articles, Internet printouts, and his own notes to go through. He tends to spend days reading all these, and then sits down to try to write,

having to keep sorting through these items for the idea he
remembers but can't quite lay his hands on. If only he could find
some way of sorting things, and marking up while he was reading –
for example, highlighting important points – he would find the
whole thing less of a drag!

Susan gets overloaded

Susan, as we have seen before, is quite organised. The only thing
that she doesn't do is manage distractions. She tends to pick
something up and start working on it right away. If anything, she
over-manages her time. One day, she was working on a report for
Harriet. She was behind, and had as usual put all her work over the
last few weeks into the day file where appropriate. She came in to
work on the report, but also then found a very large wad of papers
to be dealt with in the day file. Instantly, she was overloaded, and
knew she would never get it all done in time. She should have
checked in the day file regularly, to avoid scheduling in the report
and a lot of items in the day file at the same time.

DISCUSSION POINTS

1. Set up a day file, if you don't already have one. It may take time
    to use it effectively, but see how much more security it gives you
    in managing your workload and never missing deadlines.

2. Set up trays or areas for your reading, filing and in-tray.
    Publicise these to others, if they have work coming in, reading
    or filing for you to do.

8
Using Technology and Systems

APPRECIATING WHAT'S AVAILABLE

Today, there is a huge range of technology and systems to assist us at work, but how many of us really appreciate what is available, and how to make best use of it? Here are just some of the ways we can improve our working efficiency:

- conference calls
- e-mail
- electronic diaries
- fax computer programs
- fax machines
- laptop or portable computers
- mobile phones
- networking computers
- speaker telephones
- video conferencing
- voicemail.

Not all of these are new: some have been around for quite some time, but are being used in new ways to improve efficiency at work.

In the next section, we will list just a few of the ways in which these resources can be used to improve time management. Remember, however, that more time-saving applications are being devised all the time, so no list can ever be complete.

COMMUNICATING WITH TECHNOLOGY

Conference calls

Conference calls are telephone calls where more than two people are on the line together. They can be sophisticated, with the use of special conference call telephones, with built-in speakers and microphones, but they can also be arranged with just a normal telephone.

There are a growing number of companies which are conference call providers, but basically such calls need to be booked and set up in advance. They can be expensive, but are usually far cheaper than bringing individuals together for a meeting, or calling them all individually.

You need to remember to be very clear about what you are saying, and your meaning on a conference call. Without being able to see your body language, people have only your words to go on, and subtleties such as sarcasm, doubt, uncertainty, etc. can be lost.

How to use conference calls
Typically, when you book a conference call with a company that provides them, you will be given a number to dial in on. Everyone wanting to join the conference must dial this number, and say whose conference call they wish to join. They will then be connected to the conference call, which is exactly like a telephone conversation with many people on the line at once – which is what a conference call is! You can either speak or listen through your normal telephone handset, or alternatively, you can use a speakerphone or specialist telephone conferencing equipment, to broadcast the conversation and pick up what is said in an entire room.

Using conference calls to improve time management
- Use a conference call to avoid attending a meeting, thus saving the travelling time. It doesn't mean everyone else needs to avoid attending – you can just be conferenced in to the meeting yourself.

- Use a conference call when you have to say the same thing to several people and possibly discuss it: get them all on a conference call and deliver your message to them at once, saving you repetition time, and without anyone even needing to leave their office.

- Use a conference call instead of a meeting, thus avoiding the need of anyone to travel to the meeting. Think of this type of conference call as an audio-meeting.

E-mail

E-mail, or electronic mail, is becoming more and more common. It can save time, but it can also create almost as many problems as it solves, if not managed wisely. E-mail lets you communicate with someone anywhere in the world, sending them messages and receiving an almost instant response. It is rapidly replacing the fax as a means of communication.

One of the reasons why it is becoming so popular is because, rather than a fax receiving a printed page of paper, which may have to be retyped if it is to be used as the basis for another document, e-mail sends an **electronic copy** of the document. Therefore, when it is received, it can be viewed as with a fax, but it can also be saved, edited and used to prepare other documents, saving large amounts of typing time.

By transferring files and documents in this way, it can enormously reduce the work necessary to reproduce documents. The quality of the printed image is also not a problem – as it can be with faxed documents, especially if they have been faxed more than once, and the image deteriorates.

Using e-mail to improve time management

- Access your e-mail and check messages at certain times of the day: on the hour every hour, or every two hours – whatever is appropriate for the number of messages you receive. Resist all temptations to look between these times – you are letting yourself be interrupted by messages if you do!

- Don't, whatever you do, keep messages you have read in your in-box: it will soon become cluttered and unmanageable. Consider setting up a To Do folder for messages that require a response, as an alternative to leaving them in your in-box.

- File e-mails like other documents. Do not print them off unless *absolutely* necessary. File them electronically by subject, author, or any sensible system so you can access them and look things up as necessary.

- Learn to use your e-mail system effectively, to minimise time spent retrieving and sending messages.

- Organise the e-mails you receive, and sort them in exactly the same way as you would with incoming mail. People generally regard e-mails as urgent, just because they are there on the computer. Don't be intimidated by incoming messages. Sort them regularly as you would your in-tray: into a 'today' and a 'later' folder. Then access and deal with them at the appropriate time.

- Take advantage of the electronic nature of the e-mails you receive. You can copy and paste the text in an e-mail just as in any other computer document, so this can save you time.

- Use e-mails to avoid making telephone calls. This can save you getting caught up in conversations that would otherwise take far more time than to send a short e-mail. You needn't become a recluse, but you can use e-mail in this way to avoid getting side-tracked.

- Use e-mails to avoid correspondence. Often, companies that require a routine reply list an e-mail address. It is far quicker (and cheaper!) to e-mail a short note to them in reply, rather than writing a letter, printing and signing it, and sending it by post. You can use this to reply to invitations, to confirm details, to change contact addresses, to ask for information – anything!

Electronic diaries

Electronic diaries are becoming more and more popular. These vary from hand-held electronic organisers, which have the functions of a personal organiser in electronic format, to sophisticated compu-terised diary systems, accessible by yourself plus authorised others on your computer network.

How to use electronic diaries

Electronic diaries can be far more powerful than paper-based ones, as they can move entries around, and hold far more information. They don't get messy or clogged up with dozens of spidery handwritten notes squeezed onto the pages. But some people find them harder to use, as they aren't as visual. Some people need to have the memory aid of writing things down and reading them on paper. A big advantage of electronic diaries, however, is that they can be stored on your computer and accessed when you're out.

Using electronic diaries to improve time management

- Keep your diary in the office, and print out a copy to take with you regularly. Thus you can see your availability when you don't have access to the diary.

- Restrict access to your electronic diary to those you can trust with it! Otherwise, you will run the risk of an over-stuffed schedule. This won't cause problems if you tell people they can access it via someone, for example, a secretary, assistant or colleague. They can 'police' entries for you, and make sure you don't lose control of the diary.

- Schedule travelling time and preparation time as well as just appointments and meetings. Most electronic diaries won't allow you to enter a conflicting appointment, so this will safeguard your time for when you will need it.

- You can often add To Do lists to an electronic diary, and reminders, etc. Use the tool to its best advantage – try to use all functions, and see how useful they can become.

Fax machines

Fax machines are familiar to most of us. But very rarely do we use all the functions on our machines to best advantage. As a means of sending printed pages down a telephone line to a printer elsewhere, they are excellent, although print quality and speed can vary. They are now being more and more superseded by e-mail, for the reasons given above.

Using fax machines to improve time management

- Don't use italic type on documents to be faxed – it's harder to read when received, and can often mean you need to re-send your message.

- Set up autodial numbers for the numbers you fax most frequently.

- Set up polling lists for groups of people that you want to send the same document to.

- Stack up things to be faxed: batch them. Then have a fax session when you fax all things in one go.

- Use clean white paper with black type. It is often easy to photocopy something carelessly, leaving black marks and borders on the page. This will fax extremely slowly. Clean up your copy before faxing it.

- Use the redial! Too often people stand waiting for a fax to go. If the number you are faxing is engaged, leave the fax on the machine and trust the machine to redial – it's what it's programmed to do.

Fax programs for computers

Increasingly, computers come with a larger and larger range of software **pre-loaded**, or added to them. A common addition nowadays is a fax program. If you have this, you can use it to send and receive faxes without printing them. Just as e-mail above, this can have a number of advantages. So why would you want to use this facility?

Firstly, if you don't have e-mail, this is an improvement on a standard fax machine. Just think of not having to print your faxes, not having to stand at the machine and send them, and having improved image quality on all your faxes.

Secondly, even if you do have e-mail, if the recipient doesn't, you can fax them instead of sending them an e-mail.

Using computer fax programs to improve time management
- Don't print out documents – just send them and keep an electronic record.

- Set up address lists of groups of people you commonly send faxes to. One of the biggest advantages of a computer fax program is that you can send the same message to dozens of people at the push of a button – literally!

- Send documents at the press of a button, without having to go over to the fax machine and feed in paper.

Laptop or portable computers

Laptop or portable computers used to be used mainly by busy executives. Nowadays, their price has dropped sufficiently for them to be far more widely used. Many companies provide them for employees who travel, so they can still work and keep in touch. With a mobile telephone, you can even continue to use e-mail whilst on the move.

Many people have the best of both worlds – a desktop computer, with a laptop docking station. This means you literally plug your laptop into your desktop computer in the office.

Using laptop/portable computers to improve time management
- Copy documents you frequently need to refer to on to the laptop/portable, so you can access them any time without needing to get them faxed or sent to you.

- Take advantage of meetings and appointments away from the office. Stay on afterwards and work. People won't be able to call you unless you have a mobile phone switched on, and you will be able to work uninterrupted.

- Take a laptop/portable to meetings, appointments and training courses, etc. You can make notes, minutes, start reports, etc. straight on to the computer, doing away with the need to make written notes and copy or type them up later.

- Use waiting time and travelling time for work on your laptop.

- Work in a controlled environment. If you have the ability to move about, as with a laptop/portable, go somewhere where you can't be interrupted to work (even at home, although this can sometimes lead to distraction and procrastination).

Mobile phones
Many people nowadays have a mobile phone. They can be a blessing or a curse – although they keep you in touch, as long as that phone is switched on, you can be interrupted, and as soon as you switch it off, you are defeating the point of carrying it!

Using mobile phones to improve time management
- If you are going to use one in a car, purchase and install a 'hands free' facility. Driving and using a mobile phone without one of these is dangerous. In any event, you should be concentrating on driving and not the telephone.

- Learn how to use the mobile's facilities – they are there to save you time and effort. Many mobile phones now have advanced facilities such as call waiting, automatic redial, and a whole host of other features.

- Set up automatic dialling. It can save a substantial amount of time looking up numbers.

- Set up a divert for the phone, so when it is switched off or you are out of contact, it goes through to some form of answerphone. Most mobile service providers have this facility, but it can be time-consuming or expensive to retrieve messages. Think instead about diverting to a colleague, or to a simple answerphone.

- Switch it off when you don't want to be interrupted!

- When you don't want to be interrupted but you have a colleague you can ask, consider giving them your mobile while you attend a meeting, for example. They can take a message if the mobile rings, and interrupt you if it is so urgent that it warrants interrupting you. Too many people just switch the mobile off and return to a stack of messages, many about trivial things.

Networking computers

At work, your computer may be what is called a **standalone** machine – not connected to anything, or it can be **networked**. If your computer is networked, you can access things that other people can access and vice versa. This is called common or shared access. This can be invaluable in time management.

Using networked computers to improve time management

- Instead of sending people documents by post, fax or e-mail, you can just tell them where they are stored and they can read them for themselves.

- Print out as little as possible – it's there on the system if you need it!

- Use a password to protect documents that you want people to be able to read but not amend.

- Reduce the need for (or eliminate entirely) filing systems by filing documents on the system, rather than in paper format.

- Research things rather than re-inventing the wheel: ask people if they have any information on the system before writing new information for yourself. Use what is already there as a basis to save yourself time.

- Store documents in a place where everyone who needs to can find them, named obviously, to enable easy access.

Speaker telephones

Nowadays, an increasing number of telephones are speakerphones, or have a hands free facility. Love them or hate them, they can be very useful for time management.

Using speaker telephones to improve time management
- Ask permission to put someone on a speakerphone to let others listen in. This saves you having to pass on the message.

- Learn to use them – you need to know how to **mute**, or stop something being broadcast.

- Put someone on the speakerphone so your hands are free to take notes, even to type up the conversation as you speak. This saves you writing things up later.

- Put someone on a speakerphone if their conversation is trivial or allows you to get on with other things. For example, routine conversations from friends can be conducted while your hands are free to tidy a desk, staple documents, punch holes, whatever!

- Use a speakerphone to listen to your voicemail messages, if you have voicemail. This leaves your hands free to note the messages, and e-mail replies as you go along, saving a great deal of time.

- You can have a secretary on a speakerphone listening in to a meeting and taking minutes, without her needing to be present.

Video conferencing

Video conferencing is now a reality. Many computers sold with a range of pre-loaded software and an internal modem have a videophone capability. As costs reduce and quality improves, it is likely that this method of communication will increase further.

The main barriers to video conferencing are cost, and the fact that it generally requires access to an ISDN phone line, which isn't as yet available everywhere.

Using video conferencing to improve time management
- Don't use video conferencing unnecessarily. It can take a lot of

time setting up equipment, waiting for the connection to be made, etc. Some managers tend to use it for routine matters, that could easily be dealt with by a conference call (audio conference).

- Use video conferencing when you need to see the other person and their body language – e.g. when their emotions or feelings may be important. Examples would be making a sale, meeting a new person, interviewing, persuading someone.

- Use video conferencing when you have groups of people split by geography. Assemble two separate meetings, and video conference them together, rather than having all people travel to one location, wasting time.

Voicemail

Voicemail is a modern variant of the humble answering machine. There are a number of variants, but basically your telephone is programmed to take messages exactly like an answering machine.

Using voicemail to improve time management
- Give people options on your message. Say something like 'you can e-mail me on ... or fax me on ...'.

- Listen to voicemail messages at regular intervals, like e-mails – in batches, not frequently throughout the day. Listening to them too frequently destroys the advantage of the voicemail – to keep you from interruptions.

- Think about a discouraging voicemail message if you really don't want to be bothered. You can record a message that you are out, but URGENT messages that cannot wait can be left after the tone. This actively discourages people from leaving messages unless they really are either urgent or important.

- Use voicemail to buy yourself time – switch it on and get on with work free from interruptions.

- Use voicemail to record messages to yourself, as reminders, while you are away from your desk.

CHECKLIST

- Don't be afraid of technology – use it to your advantage.

- Don't get time-saving communications equipment and then use it ineffectively – wasting both time and money. Learn to use what you have properly.

- Use the best form of technology for your purpose.

CASE STUDIES

Harriet has to keep checking her e-mail

One of the main reasons why Harriet is so harassed is that she doesn't prioritise. She handles all things like this – answering the telephone and interrupting what she is doing, dealing with everything in the order it catches her attention. She has a computer program that beeps whenever she has a new e-mail. She regularly stops work to look at these, and even interrupts herself dealing with old e-mails that she hasn't replied to, in order to see what the latest one is about. She needs to stop and think. Also, she could save herself a great deal of time being conferenced in on meetings, instead of running about to get from one to another.

Larry has a personal organiser – but rarely uses it!

Larry was bought a personal organiser – by Harriet – for his birthday. Both had high hopes that it would get him more organised, and he was very good about entering everything he had to do. He diarised all his deadlines and things to do, and broke his research reading, etc. down and diarised that too. Unfortunately, he switched the organiser on so rarely to check what to do, preferring instead to do what he felt like each day, that it didn't help him much!

Susan makes good use of technology

Susan also has a lot of meetings in her job, but she attends few. Usually, she is required to take minutes, which she can do by speakerphone from her office. If she misses a point, she just asks them to repeat it. Susan also uses e-mail a great deal. She has a complex but effective filing system in it – set up like a day file but with the days of the week. Each time she opens an e-mail, if she needs to deal with it by the end of the week, she files it under 'Friday', etc. Each day, she knows she needs to check what is in these electronic files to be done tomorrow, to make room in her schedule for them.

DISCUSSION POINTS

1. Go through the list of communications technology above. What do you currently have access to that you aren't using? What would greatly benefit you that you don't already have? Make a case listing all the advantages for your employer – you are more likely to be given the equipment if you can prove how much use it would be.

2. Take a close look at what equipment you currently use, and how well you use it. Are there efficiencies or techniques that you can implement to save yourself time?

9
Dealing with Problem People

ASSESSING THE TYPES OF PROBLEM PEOPLE

The world would be a very simple place indeed if it were an easy matter to analyse what sort of person someone was, and to then handle them accordingly. It would even be simpler if there were definite types of person. But there aren't. In time management terms, however, two types of people cause the majority of problems, and they are at the two extremes: perfectionists and procrastinators.

Time management is about achieving more in less time. Both perfectionists and procrastinators tend, by virtue of the nature of their personalities, to achieve less in a longer time. Although each is different, they both have problems with the same two things: achieving, and the amount of time it takes them to achieve at all.

This chapter will concentrate on these two types of people, and try to establish ways of improving yourself, if you recognise one of these characteristics in yourself. We will also look at how to handle perfectionists and procrastinators that we have to work with, or simply come into contact with. With a little help, you will find them easier to handle.

PROBLEMS WITH PERFECTIONISTS

Perfectionism can be a good thing: society has long valued accuracy, attention to detail, low error rates, etc. But it can actually interfere with your progress and work, to the overall detriment of your work. Trying to be perfect can stop you feeling satisfied and motivated. It can also prevent you from achieving at all.

Figure 6 shows the cycle of perfection.

Recognising perfectionism
- All-or-nothing thinking, or black and white thinking. This is believing there is always one right answer, if only you can find it.

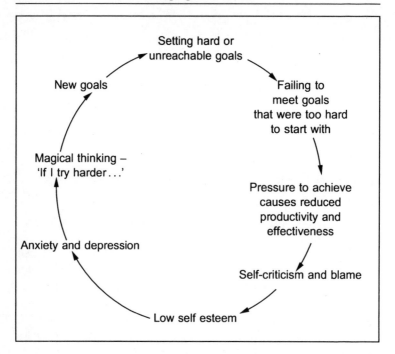

Fig. 6. The cycle of perfection.

- Being afraid of disapproval.
- Being afraid to make mistakes.
- Being over-sensitive to criticism and the opinions of others.
- Constantly looking for a mistake or slip-up.
- Difficult personal relationships.
- Difficulty keeping things in perspective.
- Equating failure with being worthless.
- Expecting too much of others.
- Feeling that what you achieve is never enough.
- Feeling you have to give 100 per cent of yourself to something or you will be a failure or something dreadful may happen.
- Living life with a set of rules: a life full of 'shoulds' and 'mustn'ts'.

- Never feeling satisfied with anything you have done.

- Putting off completing work to improve it or get it just right.

- Trying to be perfect.

- Valuing yourself based on what others think of you.

Understanding the causes of perfectionism

- Attempting to shield or protect yourself from criticism, disapproval or rejection.

- Being valued as a child or young adult for what you have achieved, rather than for being just you.

- Being shown affection or reward as a child only when you have gained approval or done something to merit it ('conditional love').

- Excessive criticism from someone who is important to you.

- Experiencing humiliation or anger from others for making a mistake.

- Having to do what is right, rather than what you want to do, for an extended period of time.

- Not being shown the effort and work behind what people do. This can lead children and young people to grow up thinking that others achieve and succeed easily, without the effort they themselves have to go to. They grow to accept their own effort as natural to 'keep up'.

Improving your own time management for perfectionists

- Accept you can't do everything to the standards you would like.

- Do things **well enough**. The only prize for consistent over-achievement is a lack of peace of mind.

- Don't be afraid to let people know you have made a mistake – or worse, attempt to cover up mistakes.

- Don't impose your high standards on others. Let them work to their own standards where possible.

- Don't set goals unless you know you can achieve them. As a frame of reference, talk them over with someone else, and if they don't think you can achieve them, re-set them. Over time you may develop more balance.

- Focus on **doing the task** as well as on the end result. Perfectionists tend to get so carried away with wanting things to be absolutely right that they lose track of the deadlines.

- Learn from mistakes. Think about how to improve as a result of making them. This may in time lead to your viewing mistakes positively.

- Prioritise. As you can't do everything, pick the things that are most important to spend most of your time on.

- Set goals based on past achievement. This increases the likelihood of you setting realistic goals.

- Set goals based on what you want and need, not what others want and need. This will give you reward for achievement.

- Set sequential goals. Start off easy, and when you have achieved, only then increase the difficulty of your goal.

- Work to reduced standards. Choose a task and work to achieve only half of it, or 75 per cent. Experiment. You may come to realise that if you don't achieve what you set out to do, nothing awful happens after all!

Working with perfectionists

- Ask them to help you set *your* goals, so they can see how others motivate themselves and think.

- Be approachable, so they are encouraged to admit to mistakes and not cover them up.

- Be careful of rewarding over-achievement. This can feed the perfectionism and encourage it.

- Check regularly that they are progressing in the right direction. Stop them focusing on quality at the expense of getting the job done.

- Discuss your own mistakes openly, and constructively. Make light of them. This will let them know that mistakes are not to be feared.

- Don't let their high standards and goals rub off on others too much. A healthy improvement in standards is good, but it can encourage perfectionism in others, which is often not a good thing.

- Encourage them to set goals based on past performance, not their best hopes.

- Help them set goals, and make sure they are realistic.

- Let them know what standard is required. Actively discourage working to exceed the required standard more then occasionally.

- Never laugh at them or criticise for lack of success or making mistakes.

- Openly discuss priorities, and ensure they are working to the right ones.

- Reward effort as well as achievement, so they can see being perfect isn't necessarily the right way to gain approval.

PROBLEMS WITH PROCRASTINATORS

Recognising procrastination
- Accepting low standards.

- Being easily distracted.

- Dawdling.

- Getting on with trivia and minor tasks to avoid or delay starting important ones.

- Getting side-tracked.

- Ignoring things in the hope they will go away.

- Indecisiveness.

- 'Just one more minute' syndrome – and then I'll start...

- Letting low priority tasks get in the way of high priority ones.

- Overcommitting yourself: taking on too much.

- Putting things off until later.

- Setting conditions before you can start; tidying desk, quiet environment, cup of coffee, etc.

- Underestimating the effort or time needed to achieve a task, even though it is obvious.

- Waiting until you're in the mood.

Understanding the causes of procrastination

- Anxiety over people's expectations of you.

- Being overwhelmed by the amount to do – excessive workloads being taken on or imposed on you.

- Fear: of success, of failure, of jealousy, of the unknown, etc.

- Inability to see how to break tasks down into small manageable chunks.

- Inability to do the task without going to others for help.

- Lack of information.

- Lack of interest or relevance. If you aren't interested in something, it can be hard to get motivated.

- Lack of motivation – being unhappy about work, looking to change jobs, etc., not believing the task should be done, or that you should do it.

- Laziness.

- Perfectionism.

- Poor time management.

- Stress. Worry about having to achieve can make it hard to get started.

- Uncertainty about what is required.

- Unclear objectives or goals.

- Unmanageable or overwhelming workloads.

Improving your own time management for procrastinators

- Accept failure and learn from it.

- Get a feel for what's involved in a task; write down all the steps.

- Get organised. Get everything you need ready before you start. But beware that you aren't using this as a means of delaying actually starting.

- Monitor your progress, with a ticked list or progress chart. This will give you a sense of achievement and enable you to achieve more because it will motivate you.

- Prioritise work and set deadlines for sub-tasks as well as for achievement of the overall task.

- Question your motives. Are you really trying to use rationalisation – to persuade yourself that it's OK to delay starting or getting on with something?

- Reward yourself for progress – for example, a cup of coffee and five-minute break for every hour working.

- Set stage goals for each stage of a task, not just for the overall task itself.

- Take regular breaks – but don't use these to put off getting the job done!

- Think positive thoughts, such as: 'Get it out of the way', 'No time like the present', 'Work now, play later'.

- Work on your weaknesses.

- Work somewhere free from distractions.

Working with procrastinators

- Compliment and encourage them when they *do* make progress.

- Don't let them get distracted.

- Don't make light of their procrastination, for example, laughing at their putting things off. This actually *rewards* them for the behaviour you want to discourage.

- Help them break down large tasks into phases or sub-tasks.

- Monitor their progress, and let them know they are being monitored. It will motivate them to get on with it.

- Nag them (nicely)!

- Reward them for progress.

- Set deadlines – for sub-tasks as well as main tasks.

QUESTIONS AND ANSWERS

Is perfectionism really such a bad thing – surely it improves the standard of work done?

It's true that a little perfectionism can work wonders. A section of staff who have got into bad or sloppy habits can be made to improve by a little injection of perfectionism. But perfectionism isn't normal thinking – it's faulty thinking. A perfectionist's beliefs and feelings are inaccurate. They cause stress levels in their own lives, and in those around them. Appropriate working is far more valuable than perfectionism to any company.

I know I procrastinate, but as long as I get the job done, what's the problem?

You could say none, but procrastination is like perfectionism – it's faulty thinking and feelings. You are being dishonest to yourself when you say lies, such as 'I'll do it after this cup of coffee', knowing you won't. These stresses and strains on your emotions can cause long-term damage.

MANAGING INTERRUPTIONS

Interruptions are a part of life. It's hard to avoid them, as they wouldn't be interruptions if we knew when to expect them! It's best to allow some time for them, as they are so inevitable.

Here are some suggestions for managing interruptions. Managing the telephone in particular can save or waste you a great deal of time. The telephone will therefore be dealt with separately in detail, in the next chapter.

Giving hints to others

- Don't smile and look welcoming. This may be hard, and seem unfriendly, but you need people to understand you are busy.

- Look briefly at your watch or a clock. This can be impolite or even rude, so be careful, but a quick look at the clock or a watch as soon as someone says 'are you busy?', or 'have you got a minute?' *before* you say 'yes, what is it?' can work wonders! It implies you really don't have long, so they need to be brief.

- Set an 'open door' time. This is a publicised time when you will be available, and when people can drop in. It discourages them from coming at other times, or if they do, you can politely ask if it can wait for the 'open door' time.

- Stand up when someone is talking to you. It discourages them from sitting down, and implies that you are on your way somewhere and can't be delayed too long.

- Walk about. There is a management technique called MBWA – Managing By Wandering About. It means wander about and get out and see people, so if they need you, they can catch you then and there and you can deal with things at your convenience. If you walk about and are approachable regularly, people won't need to interrupt you apart from with real emergencies that can't wait. But be sensitive: MBWA is basically interrupting *them*, before they can interrupt *you*!

- When someone approaches you, don't stop what you are doing at once. Make them wait for a few seconds, thus giving them the hint that they are stopping you working. It's a good idea even to say 'hello' *before* looking at them, as it implies they are taking your attention away from what you were doing.

Giving visual clues
- Close the door.

- Create visual barriers – something between you and the door. Plants or cupboards, a screen, etc. are ideal.

- Don't sit facing an open door – it *invites* people to come and interrupt you!

- Have few (or no) free seats by your desk to discourage people. They won't stay for long if they have to stand up.

- Put a 'do not disturb' notice on the door!

Taking practical actions
- Allow time for interruptions – they are almost inevitable.

- Co-operate with colleagues. Get them to answer your calls for you so you can work interrupted, in return for a reciprocal arrangement when *they* need to work.

- Get out of your office and work somewhere where you won't be interrupted.

- Say 'no' – politely.

- Work earlier or later to avoid interruptions. See whether you can 'flex' your day to start and finish early, or start and finish late. Early morning and late evening are times when there are few interruptions.

CHECKLIST

- Be sensitive with perfectionists and procrastinators, if you have to work with them.

- Look for signs of perfectionism in yourself. Ask yourself whether such behaviours are appropriate.

- Look for signs of procrastination in yourself. Ask yourself whether such behaviours are appropriate.

- Give people clues that you don't want to be interrupted. If they ignore them, use techniques to deal with their interruption quickly.

- Remember to be polite, even if you have to be ruthless with your time and be unwelcoming and unfriendly on occasion.

CASE STUDIES

Harriet avoids her boss's calls

Harriet is totally unable to deal with interruptions. She needs to use cues, and also to stop her butterfly brain getting distracted by the latest thing that happens. When she is writing a report, she stops to deal with visitors, incoming e-mails and telephone calls. She tried ignoring interruptions, but found it unsuccessful. One day when she was working on an important report, she came in to a stack of messages from her boss, wanting to see her. She ignored them, as she knew he would just be chasing the report, and it wouldn't be finished until the next day. She got fed up of him calling her, and she had Susan answer her phone to avoid him, so she managed to go the whole morning without speaking to him. Eventually, she went home after lunch and finished the report there, in relative peace and quiet (Larry went for a walk). The next day, she came in triumphantly with her report, only to discover that her boss had been trying to tell her it wasn't needed for another week. She resolved always to take calls and messages when they arrived in future. If only she hadn't over-reacted, she might have been able to work effectively that day.

Larry tells tales

Larry procrastinates. Part of him knows he does it, but another part really believes all the fairy tales he tells himself. He has to take a walk to clear his head. He needs coffee because the caffeine will stop him feeling sleepy. He can't read for too long as it wouldn't all go in. The list of excuses is endless. He should really look at *why* he is procrastinating. If he realised this, he would have the key to managing it.

Susan strives for perfection

Susan is a bit of a perfectionist. Her numerous attempts to organise Harriet have shown this before. She finds it hard to accept that she can't achieve all that she has to do – especially with Harriet messing up her schedule and working day all the time. Her stress and distress is caused by an outside influence she can't control – Harriet. What she *can* control is her own feelings and thoughts. A little less perfectionism would make everything seem less overwhelming.

DISCUSSION POINTS

1. Look carefully through the signs of perfectionism. How many can you see in yourself? How can you work on this situation?

2. Look carefully through the signs of procrastination. How many can you see in yourself? How can you work on this situation?

10
Helping Others Manage *Their* Time

MANAGING MEETINGS

Meetings can be torture! All too often, we spend valuable time sitting in meetings that we don't really need to be at, or that we *do* need to be at, but that don't serve our purposes. So how can we handle meetings to best assist us with time management? It seems simple – go to as few as possible (only those we *need* to go to), and stay as short a time as possible. But this is far easier said than done. Let's look at the most common problems with meetings, and see how to avoid them.

Planning – before the meeting

Aimless meetings – lack of objectives/purpose
Meetings need to have an objective. All too often, we go to meetings not knowing why we're there, or what the meeting is for. This is the fault of the person convening the meeting. Meetings have only three purposes:

- to discuss

- to decide or

- to inform.

Be clear about why you are convening your own meetings, and if someone is asking you to attend one, ask them *why*. Without an objective, people can't decide whether to attend or not, and they can't prepare adequately.

Attending unnecessarily
Always check meetings, and cancel unnecessary ones. Check whether meetings organised by others that you are to attend are still taking place. This is especially important if they were scheduled

a long time ago and you have not had contact with the person organising the meeting recently.

Bad agendas

The agenda can make or break a meeting. All too often, agendas consist of a shopping list of bare headings, with little or no explanation about them. As with the meeting itself, each item on an agenda should have only three reasons for being there – to discuss, to decide or to inform. Always prepare agendas for your meetings, and when you do, add a short description of each item. For example:

1. Sales figures. Go through recent sales figures for last quarter, and decide on actions to improve future performance.
2. Administration. Discussion of requirements, so appropriate staffing can be arranged.

See how much better this is than just:

1. Sales figures
2. Administration

A good agenda can help you decide whether to attend, and what you need to tell people if you can't attend, so that things can proceed in your absence without your views, opinions and input being missed. It also enables you to prepare adequately for meetings you are attending.

Another important point is to take care what order you put agenda items in. If you put the most important items first, it will encourage people to come on time. Least important matters should be left to the end of the agenda, and if the meeting is taking longer than planned, these can be postponed for a future meeting, or abandoned altogether. Often, the least important agenda items take up the most time, as they are discussed in detail. Putting these items at the end will discourage this.

Lack of preparation

People don't prepare for meetings not just because they are too busy, or can't be bothered. Often it is because they don't know how: they don't know what is required of them. A good agenda will cure this. In fact, the preparing of a good agenda is itself the best preparation a chairperson of a meeting can make.

The people present (or absent!)

Absent people

If a meeting needs input from someone who isn't there, it can delay things considerably, and can even lead to fruitless discussion about something that will change when you do get the information you need, and may even be incorrect without it. This can waste a lot of time. Check that important people will attend before the meeting, and make a judgment about cancelling or rescheduling if necessary. Consider calling people from the meeting for the input you need from them, if they can't physically be present. Or alternatively, get a briefing on the necessary information beforehand from them.

Too many people present

Meetings with too many people there tend to be hard to control. Discussions take longer, and quite simply, the more people, often the more time! Only have the right number of people at a meeting. If people only need to come for part of the meeting, schedule the agenda carefully, so everyone is there at the start, and numbers reduce as people leave after their items have been dealt with. This saves their time, as well as the meeting's.

Wrong people present

Having people present who don't need or want to be there can waste time. They may get involved in unnecessary discussions, prolonging the meeting, but also, you are wasting their own time. When you have people present who don't have the information you need, however, this is a different problem. You may have invited someone to attend, thinking they will be able to give input on a particular point, but it turns out that you should have invited someone else. This can be avoided by detailed agenda notes – so people know in advance that they aren't the best person to attend, and can suggest an alternative person.

Unhelpful behaviour

People in meetings can misbehave! They digress, they ramble on and on, they don't pay attention, they argue pointlessly over little details, they interrupt, they even fall asleep! You owe it to others in a meeting to keep to the point and try not to abuse people's time. You also owe it to people to try to stop unhelpful behaviour, which only wastes everyone's time. Be assertive, and ask politely that people keep to the point. If necessary, take a break and come back to the meeting in five or ten minutes. During the break, you can take people to one side and privately deal with the problem – ask them to be more considerate.

Assuming you have to be present or absent
It's funny, but people do tend to assume that you either go to a meeting or you don't. They forget that you can 'drop in' for just one item on the agenda, or even call in by telephone. If you have the technology, you can use a conference call facility, and have the meeting by telephone with everyone not being physically present. Or you can simply use a telephone call with someone who can't be present, and call them whenever their input is required. This means they don't have to leave their office, but they are 'on tap' when you need their expertise or advice.

The meeting itself

Unnecessary meetings
I'm sure you must have been to at least one meeting where you wondered why on earth it was happening. Unnecessary meetings are nothing but a waste of time, and you should avoid them whenever you can. They often occur because people fall into the habit of having regular meetings, e.g. weekly team meetings. These meetings then become habitual, almost traditional, and they keep occurring every week, regardless of whether they are needed. Schedule meetings only when necessary, and don't be afraid to cancel regular meetings if there isn't anything to discuss, decide or inform.

Poor control/chairmanship
Poor chairmanship/control of meetings causes problems. Mischievous or bad-mannered people will misbehave, as above, if they're allowed to – it's human nature. If a chairman of a meeting you are in doesn't control things properly, don't be afraid to step in and point out what isn't helpful. Admittedly, you run the risk of undermining their authority, but equally, they might be grateful for your help/ support. In any event, your time is at stake!

Poor timekeeping
Arriving late for meetings isn't just a waste of time, it's rude and disrespectful. If not dealt with, it gives a message to others that it's all right to be late, and the problem will get worse. I have one meeting I attend regularly that I am always 15 minutes late for –

because as *everyone* is late, it has never started before I get there, and I don't want to sit there for 15 minutes wasting my time! Don't be late yourself. Plan to get there early, and then use the time constructively. You can make calls if you have a mobile or access to a telephone, or you can read, or check work. The time you gain this way is often 'quiet time' – free from the usual interruptions.

A separate issue is meetings that over-run. Most people don't notice this, as very few meetings have an end-time. Why not? You tell people when to arrive, why not tell them when they will be able to leave? Try to give an indicated end-time if possible – it allows people to plan adequately. It also enables them to decide whether they can attend: we have a psychological tendency to assume meetings will be an hour unless we have any reason to think differently. If people knew a meeting was only going to be 20 minutes, or half an hour, they might be able to attend, whereas they may not if it was a one-hour meeting. So give them the information they need to decide.

Taking minutes
Just like holding meetings, taking minutes, typing them up, and distributing them can be part of a ritual which isn't really necessary. Only take minutes if you need to – don't do it just for the sake of it, or because minutes are the usual thing to do. If you do need them, consider using a laptop, or having the meeting in a room with a computer to type up the minutes during the meeting if possible. This will save work after the meeting typing them up.

After the meeting

Actions to be taken post-meeting unclear
After a meeting is over, usually people have things to do as a result. One of the most common time-wasters is when several people all go away and do the same thing. This duplicates time and effort. Be clear about who is doing what, and **when by**. Often people come back to the next meeting, but the next meeting is pointless, because people haven't done what they should have as a result of the first meeting. Sound familiar? Be clear – set objectives after the meeting so everyone knows what to do.

Failure to learn from mistakes
Learn from your mistakes. If you attend meetings that are badly managed or fruitless, make your apologies and don't go. You don't

have to be impolite and say why, just say you cannot attend. If you really are needed, you can always be persuaded to change your mind. But if not, you won't be missed, and eventually, they may stop asking for your presence.

If you are convening meetings yourself, don't be afraid to tackle past problems head-on. You can always take a few minutes at the beginning of the next meeting to lay down some ground rules, about how you are going to run the meetings in future. Most people will appreciate the time this will save in the long run, even if seems unnecessary at first.

COMMUNICATING IN WRITING

Communicating in writing can take a lot of your time. Streamlining your writing can save you time. So, how can you use time management in writing to your advantage?

- Answer correspondence by telephone (i.e. not writing at all!) or e-mail where necessary. These methods are both quicker and can save a lot of time. E-mails can be printed out as a record if necessary, but telephone calls provide no record of the conversation, so you may need to write a reply if you need to keep a copy, but otherwise try to write as little as possible.

- Batch work, so you deal with things in groups or batches. Plan to have a session writing letters, and a separate session writing e-mails, and another working on long reports/documents/proposals, etc.

- Consider using a dictaphone or portable cassette recorder. Often we can dictate writing into a machine while travelling on a train, in a hotel, whilst walking – at all sorts of times. This can then be typed up by yourself, a colleague, secretary, or even a typing or secretarial agency.

- Keep writing short. It takes less time to read fewer words, so your readers will save time too. Try to say everything you need on one side of paper or less. The amount of both writing and reading time that this saves will be enormous.

- Learn keyboard skills if you don't already have them. Typing can be done at speeds far greater than handwritten work, and so can save a lot of time. If you write your own work, then get it typed, and if you can change to just typing it straight on to a computer yourself, you will save an enormous amount of time. Speed will build up over time – and it's surprising how many managers still type with only two fingers, and achieve quite an acceptable speed with practice.

• Modern technology means that dictating into a computer and seeing your words typed up on the screen is a reality, not science fiction. Simple computer programs are available for around £100–£200, which can allow you to dictate direct onto a computer via a headset microphone. Such programs mean an initial investment of work, as you will need to teach the computer your voice, by reading a series of test passages, and training it to recognise your punctuation. This will initially be time-consuming, but as we said right at the beginning, you have to invest time, to save time. The rewards in the long run will be quite enormous.

QUESTIONS AND ANSWERS

I attend quite a few meetings that could do with improvement – but unfortunately, I'm not in a position to do this as they aren't 'my' meetings. What can I do about that?

It depends on the situation. You could always talk to the chairperson, and point out the improvements you think could be made. You could 'volunteer' to run the meeting, or take the minutes and do the agenda, etc., if this would help. Finally, you can suggest a 'roving chair'. This is where everyone takes turns in chairing the meeting and doing the agenda, etc. You could go first, and in your turn, make the changes you want. Hopefully, people will see the improvement and follow suit.

I have a lot of correspondence to do. How can I streamline this?

There were a lot of suggestions above. Try talking to others as well, and ask them how they manage. You can learn a lot from this. Can a secretary or junior take notes for you, or do some typing for you? Have you thought of having a range of 'standard letters' that you can use with minor alteration, instead of composing new letters each time? Be inventive.

HANDLING THE TELEPHONE

The telephone is a powerful tool for managing your time. But it can be your worst enemy at times. You need to learn to use it appropriately to take advantage of the benefits it gives you, whilst avoiding or minimising its drawbacks.

Common problems with telephone calls
- The other person rambles, won't get to or stay on the point.

- The person isn't available.

- They can't answer you because they don't know.

- They can't deal with your query.

- They don't call you back.

- They don't have the information available.

- They say 'can I call you back?'

- You are put on hold.

Having a system
This may seem a strange heading. After all, you just pick up the phone and dial, right? You don't need advice on how to make a phone call – or do you? Consider the following hints and tips. They're all common sense when you look at them individually – but how many of them do you actually do?

1. Batch your calls
- Don't procrastinate. Difficult calls, or ones you really don't want to make, must be handled in their turn – that's the whole point of the list!

- Have a list and work through it.

- If someone isn't there, go on to the next call, and keep going until you are finished.

- If you are asked if you would like to hold, don't – it wastes time. Call back.

- Make calls in blocks. This tends to 'sharpen' your conversations, keeping you brief and to the point.

- Then go back to the ones whose line was engaged, or who weren't there.

2. Prioritise calls

- Don't call too early – it catches people before they have settled into work, and may encourage more social chit-chat. Or they may not be thinking clearly enough to deal with your call.

- Don't call too late – people will give you short shift if they are in a hurry to get home.

- If calls are minor or administrative, don't make them. Delegate large batches of routine calls such as to arrange meetings, check attendance, get papers sent to you, etc.

- Make calls that require people to take action early in the day – not at the last minute. This gives them a chance to do what you want.

- Make the hardest calls first, then the others won't seem so bad, and you won't delay and try and avoid making the difficult one!

- Make the most important first.

3. Prepare in advance

- Don't call whilst eating or drinking. This sounds obvious, but it's surprising how often it happens!

- Have the numbers to hand. Fiddling about going to and from an address book (or even more than one), and looking for business cards and numbers wastes time. If necessary, get a junior to look up and list the numbers for you.

- Know why you are calling, and what you want to say. This will avoid 'beating around the bush'. It will help you get to the point.

- Make an agenda for the call if you need to cover more than one or two points. That way, you won't forget anything. Also, if you get a voicemail or answering machine, you will be prepared to leave a perfect message.

- Rehearse if the conversation is a difficult one.

4. Say why you are calling as quickly as possible

- If you are returning someone's call, say so as soon as possible. This will give them a chance to remember what they called *you* about, and if you are dealing with a secretary or assistant, they are more likely to put you through.

- In other cases, if you say immediately why you are calling, this

will give them an opportunity to say early on in the conversation
if they can't answer or help you, and you won't spend a long time
finding that out.

5. Control the conversation

- A **small** amount of small, social talk may make the other person
  more friendly, receptive and co-operative.

- Ask whether the other person has time to talk. Better to find out
  straight away if they don't rather than getting halfway through
  your explanation and being cut off by them saying they will have
  to call you back.

- Avoid being drawn into small talk, or chit-chat unless you can
  afford the time.

6. What to do if they need time to think or find out information

- If they will be able to help you, but not right now, make an
  appointment to call them back, and ask them to note it in their
  diary so they are available.

- There's nothing wrong with making a telephone appointment just
  as you would a meeting appointment to go and see them.

7. Don't rely on people

- Don't rely on someone calling you back. Most people are reliable,
  but calls can be forgotten, and mistakes made.

- If they aren't there, or if they need time to respond, call them
  back.

8. Leave sensible, meaningful messages

If you need to leave a message, make sure you give the five Ws:

- **who** you are

- **when** you called – time and day

- **what** you want

- **when** you will call back (or when they can call you)

- **what** number you can be reached on.

CHECKLIST

- Communicate in writing efficiently.

- Go to as few meetings as possible, and stay as short a time as possible!

- Make sure meetings have the right people in them – and not the wrong ones.

- Prepare for meetings properly – including setting good agendas.

CASE STUDIES

Harriet runs from one meeting to another

Harriet goes to too many meetings. What's more, she organises half of them, and makes the appointments far too close together in her diary. She therefore runs from one meeting to another, often holding up others who have to sit and wait for her to come and start the meeting. She could conference in to many of them, or let someone else chair them for her – that way if she were to be delayed, they could start without her.

Larry needs to be more disciplined

Larry never has meetings, working from home. He does have to make telephone calls, however, and ends up spending quite a lot of his time on this. A more organised, disciplined approach to his calls would save him a great deal of time.

Susan can still learn

Susan, as we have seen, is pretty well organised, but not perfect. She could still benefit from many of the techniques in this book – as can we all!

Glossary

Batching. The process of doing tasks in groups.

Clutter. A mess or disorder that interferes with other things.

Conference call. A meeting held on a telephone line, with many callers on the line at once.

Day file. A file to keep things that are needed on a particular date for easy reference.

Delegation. Giving someone else the authority to carry out part of your job on your behalf.

Effectiveness. Being productive, being capable of achieving. Doing or focusing on the right things.

Efficiency. Functioning effectively with the least effort. Doing things in the right way.

E-mail. Electronic mail. A computerised message and communication facility.

Filing. Storing documents in files for future easy reference.

Goal. A target you or someone else sets for yourself to aim at.

Perfectionism. A natural tendency to focus on the quality of things, and to aim for very high, unrealistic or perfect standards.

Procrastination. Putting off something consistently, usually by indirect, false or dishonest means.

Speakerphone. A telephone with hands free facility.

Tickler file. Another name for a day file.

Voicemail. An in-built telephone facility to take messages, like an answering machine.

Further Reading

How to be a better manager, Jane Smith (Kogan Page/Industrial Society)

Get organised, Odette Pollar (Kogan Page)

The complete idiot's guide to managing your time, Jeff Davidson (Alpha Books)

Starting to Manage, Julie-Ann Amos (How To Books)

Managing Yourself, Julie-Ann Amos (How To Books)

Index